D0196684

# FEZ

## ENCOUNTER

**VIRGINIA MAXWELL**
**HELEN RANGER**

Fez Encounter

**Published by Lonely Planet Publications Pty Ltd**
ABN 36 005 607 983

| | |
|---|---|
| **Australia** | Head Office, Locked Bag 1, Footscray, Vic 3011 ☎ 03 8379 8000  fax 03 8379 8111 talk2us@lonelyplanet.com.au |
| **USA** | 150 Linden St, Oakland, CA 94607 ☎ 510 893 8555 toll free 800 275 8555 fax 510 893 8572 info@lonelyplanet.com |
| **UK** | 2nd fl, 186 City Rd London EC1V 2NT ☎ 020 7106 2100  fax 020 7106 2101 go@lonelyplanet.co.uk |

This title was commissioned in Lonely Planet's Melbourne office and produced by: **Commissioning Editors** Errol Hunt, Lucy Monie **Coordinating Editor** Maryanne Netto **Coordinating Cartographer** James Ellis **Layout Designer** Jacqueline Mcleod **Assisting Editors** Penelope Goodes, Margedd Heliosz, Evan Jones **Managing Editor** Katie Lynch **Managing Cartographer** Shahara Ahmed **Cover Designers** James Hardy, Yukiyoshi Kamimura **Project Managers** Craig Kilburn, Chris Love **Series Designers** Nic Lehman, Wendy Wright **Managing Layout Designers** Adam McCrow, Celia Wood **Thanks to** Carolyn Boicos, Emma Gilmour, Geoff Howard, Laura Jane, Marg Toohey

**Cover photograph** Royal Palace of Fes, Franck Fuiziou/Agefotostock. **Internal photographs** p54, p78, p86, p94 by Helen Ranger. All other photographs by Lonely Planet Images, and by Doug McKinlay except p4 Izzet Keribar; p6 Olivier Cirendini; p97 Dushan Cooray.

All images are copyright of the photographers unless otherwise indicated. Many of the images in this guide are available for licensing from **Lonely Planet Images:** www.lonelyplanetimages.com.

ISBN 978 1 74179 258 4

Printed by Hang Tai Printing Company, China.

# HOW TO USE THIS BOOK
## Colour-Coding & Maps
Colour-coding is used for symbols on maps and in the text that they relate to (eg all eating venues on the maps and in the text are given a green fork symbol). Each neighbourhood also gets its own colour, and this is used down the edge of the page and throughout that neighbourhood section.

## Prices
Multiple prices listed with reviews (eg €10/5 or €10/5/20) indicate adult/child, adult/concession or adult/child/family.

**Send us your feedback** We love to hear from readers – your comments help make our books better. We read every word you send us, and we always guarantee that your feedback goes straight to the appropriate authors. The most useful submissions are rewarded with a free book. To send us your updates and find out about Lonely Planet events, newsletters and travel news visit our award-winning website: **www.lonelyplanet.com/contact**.

Note: We may edit, reproduce and incorporate your comments in Lonely Planet products such as guidebooks, websites and digital products, so let us know if you don't want your comments reproduced or your name acknowledged. For a copy of our privacy policy visit **www.lonelyplanet.com/privacy**.

## VIRGINIA MAXWELL

Though officially based in Australia, Virginia is usually found somewhere around the Mediterranean. She has authored Lonely Planet guides to Istanbul, Turkey, Egypt, Syria, Lebanon, Italy and Spain. This is her Moroccan debut.

## HELEN RANGER

Born in the UK, Helen spent most of her adult life in Cape Town. She moved to Fez in 2004, entranced by medina magic and the Fes Festival of World Sacred Music. She teaches English to Moroccan teenagers, runs a website to fund medina restoration projects and writes from her newly restored 400-year-old traditional courtyard house.

## VIRGINIA'S THANKS

Greatest thanks go to my co-author, Helen. In Fez, many thanks to David, Bernard, Hassan, Bonnie, Mark, Meera, Cecile, Jurgen and Pauline. Thanks also to Sandy and David for the company in Meknès. In Melbourne, thanks to Peter and Max for holding the fort.

## HELEN'S THANKS

Heartfelt thanks to Virginia and everyone at Lonely Planet for great encouragement, to the wonderfully warm Moroccan people, and to all medina friends.

## THE PHOTOGRAPHER

Doug McKinlay has been a travel photographer for 20 years, having started out as a stringer in war-zone locales from Cambodia to El Salvador. Nowadays, he's a regular for *The Times*, where he often works on the travel picture desk when not travelling the world on assignment. Having grown up next to the ocean and mountains of British Columbia, he now resides in leafy Blackheath in Southeast London.

Red from tanning: coloured hides drying in the sun

# CONTENTS

# THIS IS FEZ

Visitors to Fez often talk about that magical moment when the medina suddenly becomes fabulous rather than foreign, revelatory rather than overwhelming.

The great novelist Amin Maalouf writes of uncovering the city's layers '…veil by veil, like a bride in her marriage chamber', and though most visitors resemble bashful bridegrooms on their first day in town, they're usually pretty swift to get into the connubial swing of things here, falling into a deep infatuation with all things Fassi within days.

Walking through the medina is a good case in point. On day one, you'll probably spend most of your time trying to ignore touts, dodge the crowds and sidestep donkey poo. Day two will be different, though. You'll walk around a corner and unexpectedly come upon a local housewife filling a brass pitcher at a spectacularly beautiful tile-encrusted fountain. Or you'll discover a stall where fresh rose petals are being sold, their sweet fragrance mingling with that of the spicy *brochettes* (kebabs) that are being grilled on an adjacent stand. By day three you'll come to the realisation that the call to prayer is the most evocative music you've ever heard, and that the delicately carved wooden *mashrabiya* screens on the neighbourhood *medersas* (theological schools) are the most gorgeous architectural detail you've ever encountered. By day four the die will be well and truly cast: you'll be irrevocably and lastingly in love.

Here, the travel experience is as unexpected as it is extraordinary. You can listen to a Sufi brotherhood 'meet the face of God' through music, watch an elderly master craftsman show his young grandson the proper way to hand-stitch a yellow leather *babouche* (slipper), or get lost in labyrinthine lanes that have hardly changed appearance over a millennium.

Put simply, getting the most out of Fez is easy. The difficult part is leaving.

---

**Top left** A walk in the medina (p34) **Top right** Talaa Kebira (p10) **Bottom** Bab Bou Jeloud (p39)

# >HIGHLIGHTS

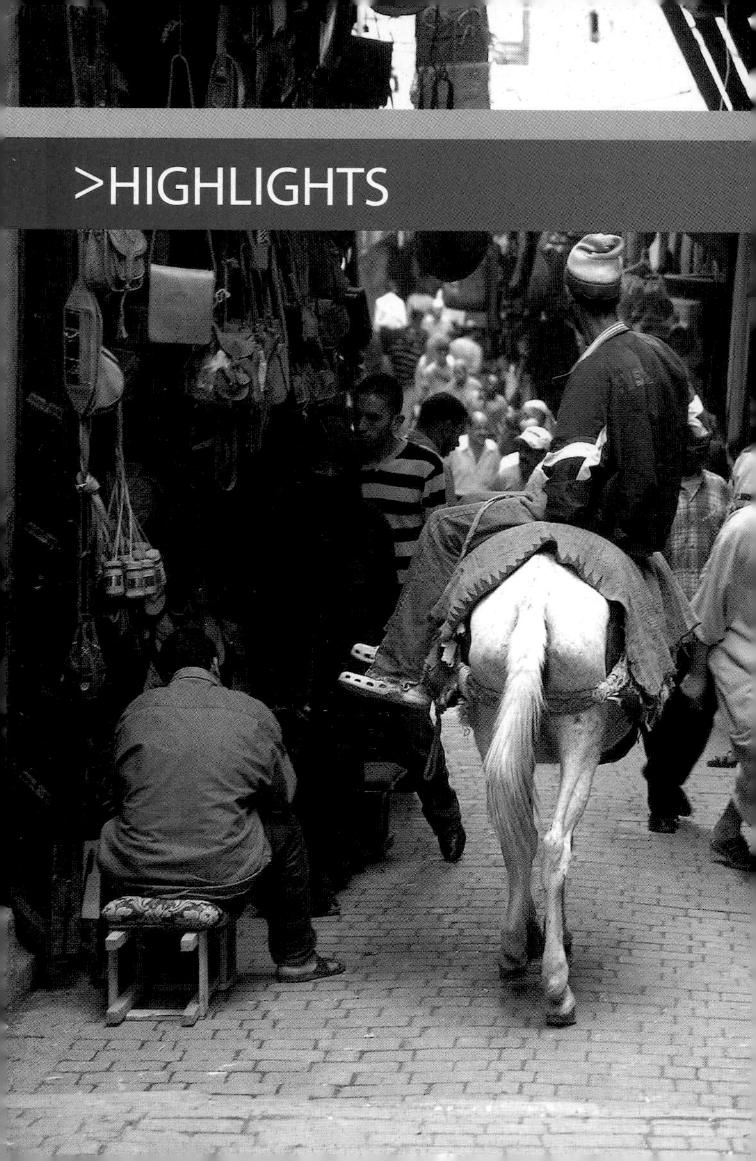

Passing parade on busy Talaa Kebira (p10)

# >1 TALAA KEBIRA

## WANDER ALONG THE MEDINA'S LONGEST AND MOST EVOCATIVE STREET

Talaa Kebira (the big slope) is the steady pulse of the city. Starting near Bab Bou Jeloud (p39), this narrow and winding artery makes its long way down towards the Kairaouine Mosque (p47), the true heart of Fez. Along its length are major monuments such as the Bou Inania (p41) and Attarine (p38) Medersas, the Chrabliyine Mosque (p42), the Nejjarine Wood Museum (p48) and the Moulay Idriss Zawiya (p48), as well as shops, *funduqs* (caravanseries), souks, hammams, fountains, cafés, markets and street stalls. The street is a mirror of Fez and its rich history – its buildings span many historical periods and styles, its residents and workers go about tasks that have been conducted for centuries and the tourists who spend hours walking its length are in many ways its – and the city's – lifeblood.

As you walk down the street you'll pass through a progression of historic artisanal clusters: slipper makers at Chrabliyine, blacksmiths at Haddadine, school-bag makers at Chkakriyine, nails at Derraqine, cobblers at Terrafine, woodworkers at Nejjarine and coppersmiths on the other side of the Kairaouine Mosque at Seffarine. Within these clusters tradesmen work with needle, thread and paintbrush, as well as with chisel, lathe and hammer. They wield these tools the way their fathers (and their fathers' fathers') taught them and their output is sold in diminutive shops and sprawling souks that have been trading for centuries. This truly is living history.

The best way to explore is simply to wander; you'll find gems down alleyways, around corners and inside many rundown buildings. Mercantile centres such as the Funduq Kaat Smen (p45) are strictly geared towards local needs, whereas other outlets clearly concentrate on snaffling the tourist dirham. Both have their proper place in the scheme of things.

This is an area that rewards proper and prolonged investigation, so make sure you allow enough time. If you get thirsty along the way, mint tea and coffee can be had at the Nejjarine Museum Café (p71), Café Kortoba (p69) or Café Ba Bouchta (p69). Café Clock (p64) is a lovely place for lunch.

## >2 FES FESTIVAL OF WORLD SACRED MUSIC

**ATTEND ONE OF THE WORLD'S BEST MUSIC FESTIVALS**
In life there aren't too many opportunities to rub shoulders with rock stars, gospel choirs, Columbian shamans, Tibetan monks and Sephardic singers. This is one of them. Held in the beginning of June, this wildly popular nine-day festival is on the A-list of international cultural events, but it's also a resolutely local affair, with free daily concerts in Bou Jeloud Sq and sensational Sufi nights at Dar Pacha Tazi (p44) where the brotherhoods make amazing music and work themselves into trances. If you're fortunate enough to score tickets to the headline events, you'll hear artists of the calibre of Ravi Shankar, Angelique Kidjo and Youssou N'dour perform in atmospheric venues including the balmy garden of the Batha Museum (p40), the grand Bab al-Makina at Moulay Hassan Sq (p80) and a Merinid quarry just outside the ancient city ramparts.

# >3 MAGNIFICENT MEDERSAS

## MARVEL AT THE ARCHITECTURAL SPLENDOUR OF THE CITY'S HISTORIC THEOLOGICAL COLLEGES

In a city with such an overindulgence of architectural masterpieces, a building needs to be pretty special to stand out from the crowd. And that's exactly what a clutch of *medersas* (theological colleges) in the medina and Al-Andalous do. These buildings showcase the very best of Fassi workmanship, sporting delicately carved plasterwork, intricately carved *mushrabiya* screens, carved and painted cedarwood ceilings and vivid *zellij* (mosaic tilework). It was during the construction of monuments such as these that Fassi artisans developed and refined the techniques that have subsequently been passed down through the generations and become famous throughout the world.

Supreme among the *medersas* is the fully restored and utterly wonderful Bou Inania Medersa (p41) on Talaa Kebira. Of equal cultural and architectural significance are the elegant Attarine Medersa (p38), which is currently undergoing a no-holds-barred restoration courtesy of the Arab Fund for Economic & Social Development, and the exquisite Sahrij Medersa (p84) and Sbaiyine Medersa (p85) complex in Al-Andalous. Sadly, the Sahrij and Sbaiyine complex is in such desperate need of restoration that it has been placed on the World Monuments Fund's list of the world's 100 most endangered cultural heritage sites.

## >4 SEFFARINE SQUARE

**WATCH THE MEDINA WORK WHILE SITTING IN ITS MOST INTERESTING SQUARE**

This sensational little square near the Kairaouine Mosque is easy to find – just listen for the sound of an orchestra of hammers tap-tap-tapping hundreds of copper and brass utensils into shape. Strategically located on the major route from Bab R'cif into the medina, it's populated by coppersmiths and is probably the best position in Fez for people-watching. Few activities are as enjoyable as perching on one of the stools at Cremerie la Place (p69), ordering a mint tea and watching the medina population go about its day-to-day rituals. On one side of the square is the still-functioning Seffarine Medersa (p49), the oldest Merinid *medersa* in the city, and close to that is the ancient Seffarine Hammam (p73), whose clientele includes the medersa's students, the coppersmiths and local residents. On the other side of the square are the imposing doors to the Kairaouine Library (p46), the most venerable place of learning in Fez.

## >5 THE MELLAH
### EXPLORE MOROCCO'S ORIGINAL JEWISH GHETTO

Like the medina, the Mellah is old, intact, culturally significant and as far removed from a Disneyfied heritage theme park as you could possibly imagine. The city's historic Jewish ghetto, it took its name from the Oued el-Maleh (Salty River), a tributary of the Oued Fès (Fez River), and then passed the name on to similar districts in Marrakesh, Meknès and other Moroccan cities.

The area the Mellah occupies in the southern section of Fez el-Jdid was first reserved for Syrian archers in the service of the Merinids, but became home to the Jewish residents of Fez when they relocated here from the Sagha district of Fes el-Bali in the 14th century. Living under the sultan's protection, they established goldsmithing businesses in and around Rue Sekkakine (p80), built opulent mansions on Derb el-Fouqui, buried their dead in the Jewish Cemetery (p79) and erected four places of worship in the 17th century, including the Ibn Danan Synagogue (p79). Sadly, no Jews live here today.

HIGHLIGHTS

## >6 STAYING IN A RIAD

### SAMPLE THE LIFESTYLE AT A TRADITIONAL COURTYARD HOUSE

It's one thing to visit historic monuments on a sightseeing expedition, but it's an entirely different thing to actually bunk down in one at night. And this is why you'd be crazy not to stay in a riad while you're in Fez. The medina is home to a wonderful array of restored riads (traditional houses built around gardens with trees) and *dars* (traditional houses with internal courtyards) that offer intimate and superstylish accommodation for visitors. These places are resorts for the discerning traveller, offering living history and personal touches rather than swimming pools and marble lobbies. You can wake up in rooms with magnificent painted ceilings, breakfast under orange trees or next to gently playing marble fountains, listen to the call to prayer from panoramic terraces and dine on Moroccan delicacies prepared by the riad's own chef. Life doesn't get much better than this.

Check p104 for our guide to choosing the riad that's right for you.

## >7 SHOPPING

### SHOP TILL YOU DROP (OR BREAK THE BANK)

Fill your wallets and charge your credit cards. If you're a shopaholic, Fez is most certainly the place to be. We challenge you to explore every souk, suss out every bargain and still stay under the excess baggage cut-off for your flight home – we've been trying for years and reckon it just ain't possible. Best buys are *babouches* (traditional leather slippers), silver Berber jewellery, the famous blue-glazed Fassi ceramics, hand-sewn linen and cotton embroidery, Berber *hendiras* (traditional woven cloaks that make great wall hangings), argan oil (for cooking or in soap), saffron and other spices, brassware, and carpets of every type, style and quality.

Sensational shopping strips and souks are everywhere, but don't miss Talaas Kebira and Seghira, the Attarine Souks (p39), Chemmaine Souk (p42) and the *kissariat* (covered markets; p58) at the bottom of Talaa Kebira, near the Kairaouine Mosque.

## >8 HAMMAMS & SPAS

### GET HOT AND STEAMY AFTER A DAY IN THE MEDINA

After traversing the steep, dusty and uneven streets of the medina, you may well find yourself tired, dirty and aching all over. Fortunately, there's a remedy close at hand that's as enjoyable as it is effective: a session in one of the city's hammams (bathhouses) or spas.

There are loads of functioning hammams in the medina, a reflection of the fact that many houses here still don't have bathrooms. Visitors are more than welcome, but should be prepared for an invigorating rather than pampering experience. Before you go, buy a hammam mat, an exfoliating mitt and some *sabon beldi* (dark brown gelatinous soap that's great for the skin) from a souk – you'll need these for a session of *gommage* (exfoliation), massage and bath. You'll be pummelled, rubbed and drenched and will bare all with locals young and old. The cleanest of the local hammams is the Ain Azleten Hammam (p71) on Talaa Kebira, but even this place has standards of cleanliness that can be confrontingly low.

At the other end of the spectrum are the luxury spas, of which Fez has an indulgent array. In the medina try the posh Fès Palais d'Hôtes Spa Andalous (p71) or the lovely Riad Maison Bleue Spa (p73). In the Ville Nouvelle, try the sleek Nausikaa (p95) or Yubacyn Spa (p96). These spas both offer upmarket variations on the hammam ritual, as well as a range of massage, hair and beauty treatments.

# >9 FABULOUS FUNDUQS

## CHECK OUT A FEW CARAVANSERIES

In the days when Fez was a major stop on the trading routes between North Africa and the rest of the world, caravans of merchants
with their camels, horses and other livestock needed a place to base
themselves while in town. Medieval equivalents of the modern-day
motel, these *funduqs* (caravanseries) came in every possible size and
style and are scattered throughout Fez el-Bali and Fez el-Jdid, often
adjacent to souks where the goods carried by the caravans were
sold. Wealthy merchants would have parked their camels in grand
examples of the genus, such as the magnificent Nejjarine Funduq
(now the Nejjarine Wood Museum, p48) or Sagha Funduq (p49),
whereas their more modest colleagues may well have laid down
their turbans in places such as the Funduq Tazi (p45) and Funduq
Tastawniyine (p45).

HIGHLIGHTS

## >10 THE FOUNTAINS OF FEZ
### PONDER THE FASSI OBSESSION WITH FOUNTAINS

It's no exaggeration to say that Fassis have a fountain obsession. There are many opinions about why and when this originated (no doubt Freud would have formulated a theory if he'd ever visited), but the sheer number of attractively decorated public fountains (*seqqâya*) in the city's streets, souks and squares leads us to hazard a guess that they can't have all been for ablution before worship in mosques. After all, the recent beautification works on Ave Moulay Hassan II in the Ville Nouvelle have fountains as their centrepiece despite the fact that there's hardly a mosque in sight… But enough of our crackpot theories. The important thing to say here is that no visit to Fez can be complete without seeing a few examples – we particularly admire the one in Nejjarine Sq (p48).

# >FEZ DIARY

Quality rather than quantity is the rule when it comes to festivals in Fez, and it works a treat. The world-renowned Fes Festival of World Sacred Music is the city's signature performance, but warm-up acts such as the impressive new Festival of Sufi Culture and encores such as the National Festival of Berber Culture deserve enthusiastic rounds of applause, too. Best of all are the annual *moussems* (festivals or pilgrimages) of the Sufi *tariqas* (brotherhoods). These feature processions through the streets in which traditional music is played and followers dance, experience *hadra* (feeling the presence of God and entering a trance-like state) and shower the musicians with orange or rose water.

Having a blast at the Festival of Sufi Culture (p22)

# JANUARY

### National Festival of Andalous Music in Fes
**Festival de la Musique Andalouse à Fès;**
☎ **035 637228/39**
Organised by the Urban Commune of Fez, this low-key festival showcases the very best of Andalous music (see p111) through performances, colloquiums, master classes and lectures.

# APRIL

### Festival of Sufi Culture
**Festival de la Culture Soufie;**
**www.par-chemins.or**
Established and organised by Faouzi Skalli, who founded the Fes Festival of World Sacred Music, this annual festival had its debut in 2007. Venues included the magnificent Mokri Palace (see p48) and Bou Jeloud Sq.

Trance – the Sufi way – at the Fes Festival of World Sacred Music

## National Festival of Malhoun Music

### Festival National de Malhoun

Held in various venues around Fez, this festival showcases the traditional music of the craftsmen's guilds (see p111).

## Moussem Sidi Ali ben Hamdush

☎ 035 524426

This powerful *moussem* (pilgrimage and festival) is attended by thousands of followers of Sidi Ali ben Hamdush, the sheikh of the Hamadcha Sufi Brotherhood. It's held in the small village of Sidi Ali near Meknès. Note that the date changes each year according to the Islamic calendar.

# JUNE

## Fes Festival of World Sacred Music

### Festival de Fes des Musiques Sacrées du Monde; ☎ 035 740691; www.fesfestival.com

This major event on Fez's cultural calendar is one of the world's most famous music festivals. For more information see p12 and p28.

## Sefrou Cherry Festival

### Fête des Cerises à Sefrou; ☎ 035 660001/3

Held in the Berber village of Sefrou, which is 40 minutes' drive from Fez, this annual festival features folkloric displays and performances, as well as an orgy of cherry eating and the crowning of a cherry queen.

# JULY

## National Festival of Berber Culture

### Festival National de la Culture Amazigh

Run in association with the Institut Royal de la Culture Amazigh (Royal Institute of the Amazigh Culture), this festival aims to promote and protect Amazigh (Berber) culture. Its programme includes musical performances as well as lectures and workshops.

## Moussem Sidi Ahmed Tijani

☎ 035 637228/39

This vibrant three-day *moussem* in the medina celebrates the achievements of Sidi Ahmed Tijani (1737–1815), the founder of the Tariqa Tijaniya (see p110). Note that the date changes each year according to the Islamic calendar.

# SEPTEMBER

## Moussem de Sidi Lahcen el-Youssi

☎ 035 660001/3

This *moussem* in Sefrou celebrates the life of Sidi Lahcen el-Youssi, a 17th-century saint from the neighbouring village of Azzaba. Note that the date changes each year according to the Islamic calendar.

FEZ DIARY

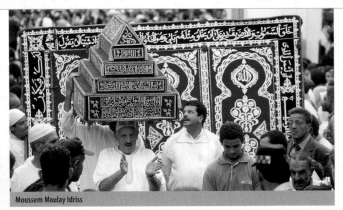

Moussem Moulay Idriss

# OCTOBER

### Fez Culinary Festival
**Festival des Arts Culinaires;**
☎ 035 740535

A three-day event run by the Spirit of Fès Foundation and the Conseil Régional du Tourisme (CRT) that hosts top-name chefs from Morocco and overseas. You can expect talks, demonstrations and tastings focussing on ingredients, cuisines and methods.

### Moussem Moulay Idriss
☎ 035 637228/39

This one-day *moussem* pays homage to Moulay Idriss, the revered founder of Fez. It's one of the most important religious festivals in Morocco. Local artisans create special tributes and there's a huge procession through the medina. Note that the date changes each year according to the Islamic calendar.

### Moussem de Sidi Ali Boughaleb
☎ 035 637228/39

This two-day celebration of Sidi Ali Boughaleb, the patron saint of barbers, is held around his mausoleum in the Al-Andalous quarter. Note that the date changes each year according to the Islamic calendar.

# NOVEMBER

### Jazz in Riads Festival
**Festival Jazz in Riads;**
**www.jazzinriads.com**

Run by the CRT and the Association of Riads de Fès, this event sees jazz musicians from all over the globe performing in wonderfully restored riads (traditional houses built around gardens with trees) and *dars* (traditional houses with internal courtyards) throughout the medina.

Remains of the Roman city of Volubilis (p100)

# ITINERARIES

## A MORNING IN THE MEDINA

Enter the medina through Bab Bou Jeloud (p39) and then wander down Talaa Kebira, stopping to visit the Bou Inania Medersa (p41). To get into the medina swing of things, stop for a caffeine fix on the terrace at Café Clock (p64), located opposite the *medersa*. Continue your perambulation down the slope, investigating the shops, souks and street stands along the way. Passing through Chrabliyine, turn right into Derb Fakharine to discover the Henna Souk (p45) and Nejjarine Sq (p50), home to the Nejjarine Wood Museum. Then through Bab Moulay Idriss to the Moulay Idriss Zawiya (p48) and on to the *kissariat* (covered markets; p58) near the Kairaouine Mosque & University (p47). Returning to Talaa Kebira, veer left (north) into Derb Rhabt l'Qaïs, through the Blida neighbourhood and then onto the Chouwara Tanneries (p42). From here, make your way to Seffarine Sq (p50) and celebrate a great morning's sightseeing over a mint tea or fresh juice at Cremerie la Place (p69).

## AN AFTERNOON IN THE MEDINA

After your morning exploring the length of Talaa Kebira catch a taxi from Bab R'cif to Batha, where you should note the location of the Batha Museum (p40) for an after-lunch visit. Lunch is first though – try Thami's (p68), a street café on Derb Serrajine. After lunch make your way back to the museum and enjoy viewing its collection before catching another taxi, this time to the Hotel Les Merinides (p70) to enjoy a drink on the terrace while watching the spectacle of the sun setting over the medina. Later in the evening, have a sumptuous Moroccan meal and enjoy listening to live music at La Maison Bleue (p65) or Riad Fes (p67).

## TWO-DAY TWIRL

Follow the itineraries above on your first day. On day two, walk or catch a petit taxi to Alaouites Sq to explore the Mellah (p15). Next, proceed through Bab Semmarine (p76) and up busy Derb Fez el-Jdid to Moulay Hassan Sq (p80). A leisurely lunch is now in order, and Café Restaurant La Noria (p81) is the perfect place for this. After lunch, make your way into

---

**Top left** Bou Inania Medersa (p41) **Top right** Buying mint among the narrow alleys of the medina **Bottom** Working the hides in the tanneries (p42)

> **FORWARD PLANNING**
>
> If you want to attend the Fes Festival of World Sacred Music, you'll need to book tickets through **Objectif Maroc** ( ☎ 035 652816) as soon as the programme is announced. Accommodation needs to be booked even earlier – a year in advance isn't unknown, six months is safe, one month means that you'll be dossing with the donkeys.
>
> Tickets for the other festivals are nowhere near as difficult to score, though once the new Festival of Sufi Culture builds an international reputation the situation could change.
>
> During the high season (Easter, Christmas, August, spring and autumn), you should be safe booking accommodation a month in advance and you might even get lucky with last-minute bookings. Restaurants don't usually need to be booked until you've arrived in town.

the medina through Bab Chems and prepare for some serious shopping on and around Talaas Kebira and Seghira. When you've blown your budget, drop your purchases back at your hotel and then move on to dinner at either Dar el-Ghalia (p65) or Dar Anebar (p65).

## THREE-DAY IMMERSION

Follow the previously suggested itineraries for your first two days. On day three walk or take a taxi to Bab Fettouh (p84) and saunter down Derb Aqbat Sidi Ali Boughaleb until you come to Derb Yasmina. Turn right to visit the Sahrij Medersa (p84) and admire the monumental entry to Al-Andalous Mosque (p84), before making your way down the winding streets to Bab R'cif where you can settle down for an extended people-watching session over mint tea and delicious pastries at Café de Tabarakallah (p69) on the edge of the medina. Suitably refreshed, make your way to the Achebine Souk (p38) and the Attarine Souks (p39) and spend an hour or so exploring and taking your pick of the street-food snacks on offer, before kicking on to the Ville Nouvelle by taxi. Join the locals promenading up and down Ave Moulay Hassan (see p91) and then move on to dinner at Les Trois Sources (p92) or Le Majestic (p91). End your evening with a few drinks at the seedy but undeniably enjoyable Le Marocain (p95).

## FOUR DAYS, TWO IMPERIAL CITIES

Follow the previously mentioned itineraries for the first three days and then hire a taxi for a day to take you to Meknès, another of Morocco's imperial cities. See the sights highlighted on p98 and then make your way home via the ruins of the ancient Roman city of Volubilis (p100). You'll be back in Fez in time to have a final Moroccan meal at Restaurant Zagora (p92) or Restaurant Marrakech (p92).

## FEZ FOR FOODIES

Some visitors come to Fez solely for the food. And once you've had a few meals here, you'll know why. Do your daily research by checking out the medina's fresh produce markets at the top of Talaa Kebira, at R'cif and at Jouteya (see p67), as well as at the Central Market in the Ville Nouvelle (p90). For lunch, take the medina's food stands by storm, sampling the many tasty treats on offer. Don't eat too much though, because you'll need to conserve your energy and stomach capacity for the fabulous feasts served up each evening by the kitchens of top-notch restaurants such as La Maison Bleue (p65), Riad Fes (p67), Dar Anebar (p65) and Dar el-Ghalia (p65).

There's no danger of spreading yourself too thin at the medina's food stands (p68)

# >NEIGHBOURHOODS

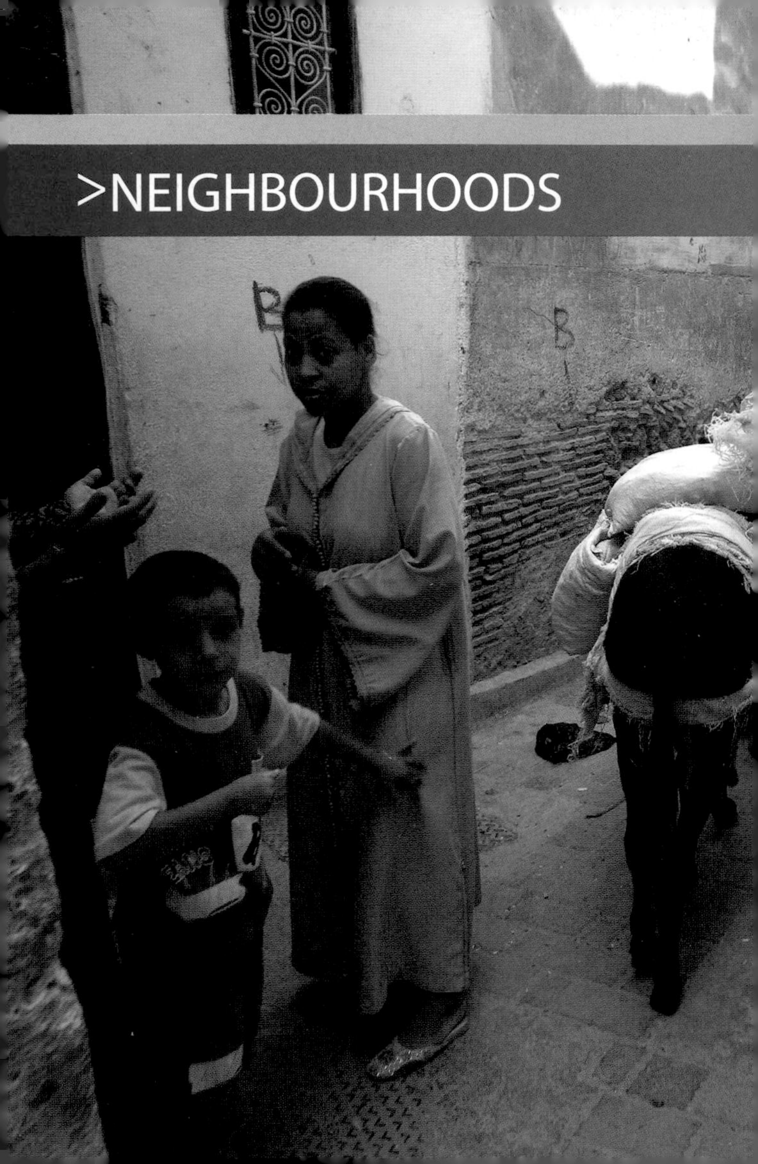

Standing back to let a medina donkey train go by

# NEIGHBOURHOODS

This is a tale of one city, four very different neighbourhoods, and over a thousand years of living, breathing history.

The two great mosques of Fez tell the story of the city's founding. Fleeing persecution in Andalusia, 8000 Muslim families made their way here in the 9th century and settled on the east side of the Oued Fès (Fez River), establishing the quarter that has ever since been known as Al-Andalous and which has as its geographical centre the Al-Andalous Mosque. Not too many years later they were joined by Muslim refugees from Tunisia, who settled on the west bank of the river and named their quarter and the mosque at its centre Kairaouine after the Tunisian city that had been their former home. Over centuries, the two quarters became known collectively as Fez el-Bali (Old Fez). In this chapter we've called the quarter to the west of the river the Medina and we have retained the descriptor Al-Andalous for the quarter east of the river. Both are warrens of twisting alleys, golden-brown houses, hidden souks and a sprinkling of grand mosques, *medersas* (theological colleges) and palaces. Together, these neighbourhoods are populated by 150,000 residents, a growing number of expats and an unknown (but considerable) number of donkeys and mules.

When the Merinids built Fez el-Jdid (New Fez) four centuries later, it was so clean and modern that the locals referred to it as Medina el-Baida (White City). It doesn't sparkle and shine these days but has retained a very distinct character, with its attractive boulevards much wider and more full of light than the medina equivalents, and its Jewish quarter (Mellah) redolent of a very different culture.

Then there's the Ville Nouvelle (New Town), with its self-consciously modern aesthetic and palpably more affluent residents. This is where the city's movers and shakers live and conduct their business, where wine is drunk and where the local bureaucracy is based. It's centuries removed from the mayhem, mystery and magic of the medina. And we mean that literally.

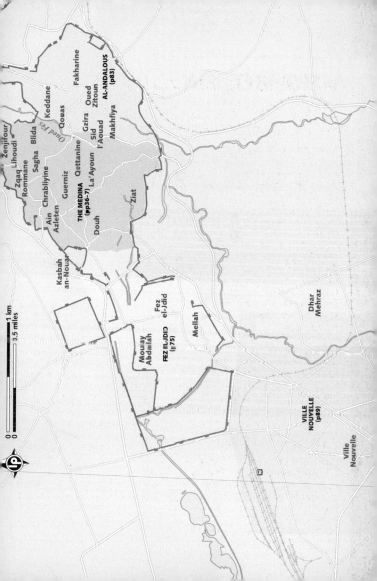

Zenjifour

Zqaq Lhoudi

Rommane

Sagha

Blida

Keddane

Fakharine

Oued

Zitoun

AL-ANDALOUS (p83)

Oued les

Ain Azleten

Chrabliyine

Guerniz

Qettanine

Gzira

Sid l'Aouad

Oued les

Makhfiya

THE MEDINA (pp36-7)

La'Ayoun

Douh

Ziat

Kasbah an-Nouar

Fez el-Jdid

Moulay Abdallah

FEZ EL-JDID (p75)

Mellah

Dhar Mehraz

0    0.5 miles

0    1 km

VILLE NOUVELLE (p89)

Ville Nouvelle

# >THE MEDINA

The main thoroughfares of the medina are Talaa Kebira (the big slope) and Talaa Seghira (the little slope) which stretch all the way from Bab Bou Jeloud in the west to the Kairaouine Mosque in the east. Along these tangled, cobbled streets you'll find most of the historic buildings, shops and souks in this quarter. The Kairaouine Mosque and the Moulay Idriss Zawiya, the mausoleum of the founder of Fez, form the heart of the medina. The city expanded outwards from these two monuments. First came the *medersas* (theological colleges) and *funduqs* (caravanseries), with adjacent souks selling goods, such as votive candles and incense, from the caravans. Beyond these were more souks with books, clothing and shoes, and artisans' workshops for making household and leather goods. Fresh produce markets and residential areas sprang up on the periphery.

## THE MEDINA

### SEE

| | | |
|---|---|---|
| Achebine Souk | 1 | G2 |
| Ain Khaïl Mosque | 2 | F3 |
| Attarine Gates | 3 | G3 |
| Attarine Medersa | 4 | G3 |
| Attarine Souks | 5 | G3 |
| Bab Bou Jeloud | 6 | C5 |
| Bab Guissa | 7 | F1 |
| Batha | 8 | D5 |
| Batha Museum | 9 | C5 |
| Belghazi Museum | 10 | F4 |
| Blacksmith | 11 | F3 |
| Borj Nord (Armaments Museum) | 12 | C2 |
| Bou Inania Medersa | 13 | C5 |
| Chemmaine Souk | 14 | G3 |
| Chouwara Tanneries | 15 | H3 |
| Dar Adiyel | 16 | F4 |
| Dar Ba Mohammed ben Chergui | 17 | D4 |
| Dar Dmana | (see 20) | |
| Dar Glaoui | 18 | F6 |
| Dar Pacha Tazi | 19 | D5 |
| Demnati Fountain | 20 | E3 |
| Diwane Mosque | 21 | G3 |

| | | |
|---|---|---|
| El-Makoudi Mosque | 22 | G2 |
| Funduq Kaat Smen | 23 | D3 |
| Funduq Tastawniyine | 24 | G3 |
| Funduq Tazi | 25 | D4 |
| Henna Souk | 26 | F3 |
| Kairaouine Library | 27 | G3 |
| Kairaouine Mosque & University | 28 | G3 |
| L'Marqtane | 29 | G2 |
| Lihoudi | 30 | G2 |
| Maristane Sidi Frej | (see 26) | |
| Merenid Tombs | 31 | E1 |
| Mokri Palace | 32 | F6 |
| Moulay Idriss Mzara | 33 | D4 |
| Moulay Idriss Zawiya | 34 | G3 |
| Nejjarine Square | 35 | F3 |
| Qbieb Naqes | 36 | G2 |
| Riyad Mokri | 37 | F5 |
| Sagha Funduq | (see 38) | |
| Sagha Square | 38 | G2 |
| Seffarine Medersa | 39 | H4 |
| Seffarine Square | 40 | G3 |
| Sidi Ahmed Tijani Zawiya | 41 | G2 |
| Water Clock | 42 | C4 |

### SHOP

| | | |
|---|---|---|
| Abdallah Ouazzani Ibrahimi | 43 | E3 |
| Alami Hassan | 44 | G3 |
| Allal Art Gallery | 45 | G3 |
| Antiquité Nejjarine | 46 | F3 |
| Art du Bronze | 47 | D5 |
| Au Coin du Bois | 48 | F4 |
| Au Petit Bazar du Bon Acceuil | 49 | D5 |
| Bachir El Meski | 50 | F3 |
| Basket Shop | 51 | F3 |
| Brassware Shop | 52 | F3 |
| Brocante Bab Touta | 53 | E3 |
| Bucket Maker's Shop | 54 | F3 |
| Card Shop | 55 | E3 |
| Chez Boutbi Nadia | 56 | D4 |
| Chez La Famille Berbère | 57 | F3 |
| Coin Berbere | 58 | D4 |
| Coin de Henne | 59 | F3 |
| Coin des Instruments Musical | 60 | F3 |
| Cooperative Artisanale (Leatherworker's Cooperative) | 61 | F3 |
| Curiosites Berberes | 62 | E4 |
| Dried Fruit Shop | 63 | G3 |

Branch off Talaas Kebira and Seghira to discover real life in this medieval city: a man with a towel on his head leaves a hammam, a child with a covered tray carries bread to the *farrane* (communal oven), a woman haggling at a stall will take that chicken she bought home, pluck it and cook it for lunch. In these streets men still embroider caftans by hand, tan hides, chisel marble, make ceramic tiles, paint pottery, shape copper basins, carve cedarwood and hammer brass trays. The main entry points to the medina are at Batha, Ain Azleten, Bab Guissa and R'cif where parking and taxis can be found. It's hilly terrain with cobbles underfoot, and is often very crowded in the late afternoon and early evening when everyone's out for a walk and a bit of window-shopping. When you hear cries of '*Andak*!' or '*Balek*!', get out of the way to let a heavily laden mule, a donkey or a man with a heavy cart pass by. You might well get lost. But fear not, you'll come across a main street pretty soon, or a friendly local will point you in the right direction.

| | |
|---|---|
| Ech Chahed Youssef | **64** D3 |
| Fès Art Gallery | **65** H3 |
| Galerie Jamil des Beaux Arts | **66** G3 |
| Galerie Nejarine | **67** F3 |
| Ghazal Miloud | **68** D4 |
| Herboristerie Bou Inania | **69** C4 |
| Kelim Berber | **70** E3 |
| Kissariat | **71** G3 |
| L'Art Bleue | **72** H2 |
| L'Art Traditionnel | **73** G3 |
| Maison Bleue (Ceramics) | **74** F4 |
| Maison d'Artisanat | **75** D4 |
| Maison des Brodeuses Fassies | **76** F4 |
| Maison Sahara | **77** F3 |
| Mat Maker | **78** D4 |
| Mister Cuir Marocain | **79** F4 |
| Najib Cuir | **80** E3 |
| Neq Broderie | **81** C5 |
| Nougat Shop | **82** F3 |
| Parfumerie Medina | **83** F3 |
| Parfumerie Moulay Idriss | **84** G3 |
| Salon de Thé Batha | **85** D6 |
| Semlali Mohamed | **86** D4 |
| Smail Wazzani | **87** E4 |
| Spice Shop | **88** D4 |
| Tissage Berbere | **89** F4 |
| Wedding Clothes Shop | **90** G3 |
| Woodwork Shop | **91** D4 |

### 🍴 EAT

| | |
|---|---|
| Bou Jeloud Market | **92** C5 |
| Café Clock | **93** C4 |
| Dar Anebar | **94** G1 |
| Dar el-Ghalia | **95** G6 |
| Dar Roumana | **96** E2 |
| Jouteya Market | **97** F3 |
| Kasbah Restaraunt | **98** C5 |
| La Maison Bleue | **99** D5 |
| Palais Jamaï | **100** G1 |
| R'cif Market | **101** G5 |
| Restaurant Bouayad | **102** C5 |
| Restaurant des Jeunes | **103** C5 |
| Restaurant Fassi | **104** C5 |
| Riad Fès | **105** E5 |
| Riad Sheherezade | **106** E6 |
| Ryad Mabrouka | **107** C5 |
| Sandwiches Big Mac | **108** C5 |
| Snail Stand | **109** E4 |
| Thami's | **110** C5 |

### 🍷 DRINK

| | |
|---|---|
| Café Ba Bouchta | **111** G2 |
| Café de Tabarakallah | **112** H5 |
| Café Firdaous | **113** D5 |
| Café Kortoba | **114** G3 |
| Cremerie La Place | **115** G3 |
| Hotel Batha | **116** D6 |
| Hotel Les Merinides | **117** D1 |
| L'Alcazar | (see 105) |
| Nejjarine Museum Café | **118** F3 |
| Palais Jamaï Hotel | (see 100) |

### ⭐ PLAY

| | |
|---|---|
| Ain Azleten Hammam | **119** D4 |
| Consul Bar | (see 116) |
| Les Musicales du Palais el-Mokri | (see 32) |
| Massage Maroc | **120** E5 |
| Parfumerie Medina | (see 83) |
| Riad Alkantara | **121** E5 |
| Riad Maison Bleue Spa | **122** D3 |
| Seffarine Hammam | **123** G4 |

Please see over for map

#  SEE

Fez is a wonderment of fascinating sights and sounds, and these form the core of any visit to the medina. There are historical monuments galore, fascinating architecture with its colour-burst *zellij* (mosaic tilework) and Arabic script, and palaces and riads to discover. But it's about more than the buildings: watch the people going about their everyday lives, in ways unchanged for centuries.

## ⊙ ACHEBINE SOUK
### Achebine, Sagha

This street formerly housed traditional medicine shops; there's one left, with jars of snakeskins, birds in cages, live chameleons, gazelle horns and skins on the walls. Nowadays it's a bird market – locals buy chickens and turkeys, doves and pigeons. There are lots of food stands here and the air is thick with smoke from *kefta* (spiced meatballs of lamb or beef) kebabs being grilled.

## ⊙ AIN KHAÏL MOSQUE
### Derb Ain Khaïl, Zqaq Rommane

Where can a camel pass under a minaret? If you know the answer to this question, you're a true Fassi. This 11th-century mosque has an octagonal minaret built over the street. The Sufi philosopher Ibn el-Arabi (1165–1240) is said to have

FEZ >38

---

### FEZ NECK
Fez Neck is a curious condition brought on by looking skywards while dropping your jaw in amazement. It's hard to avoid in the medina, where you'll be constantly looking up at marvellously carved and painted ceilings thick with 'stalactites' of painted and carved wood, wondrously intricate plasterwork, crenellated walls like fairytale castles or maybe just the storks that nest on towers. A possible cure is a hammam massage.

seen a mystical vision of intense light here. A few years ago, a badly degraded house collapsed into the prayer-hall, killing 12 men. The mosque is not in use and funding has been applied for from the EU's Euromed Heritage Programme to restore it.

## ⊙ ATTARINE GATES
There are massive wooden gates at the bottom of Talaa Kebira opposite the entrance to the Attarine Medersa (below). There used to be gates within the medina closing off every neighbourhood; these are the only intact ones left that are still closed at night, at around 10.30pm.

## ⊙ ATTARINE MEDERSA
### Talaa Kebira; admission Dh10; ⊙ 9am-6pm, closed at prayer times
Closed for extensive renovation at the time of writing but due to

open early in 2008 (*ensha'llah*, or God Willing), this *medersa* at the bottom of Talaa Kebira was built between 1323 and 1325. A favourite of students coming to study in Fez, it has unique square pillars around a *zellij*-floored courtyard with a marble fountain and a prayer-hall with a carved-wood dome, as well as Iraqi glass behind carved-plaster latticework 'windows'. There are two *zellij* panels at the entrance to the prayer-hall and two narrow galleries around the courtyard.

### ☑ ATTARINE SOUKS
**Attarine, north of Talaa Kebira**
There's a cluster of souks just off the Talaa that are worth exploring. Coming from Bab Bou Jeloud, the first is **Souk Triba**, meaning 'square in shape', with a small orange tree and some cosmetic and electronic shops. Walk through to next souk **Souk Tallis** where sacks for wool and wheat were sold. Now there's a carpet stall and several shops selling cloth for jellabas (cloak with a hood) – though many of the shops are now closed. Continue through to the next souk, **L'Hayek** ( 9am-12.30pm & 3-5pm Sat-Thu), which refers to the white cloth used for women's clothes. These days there are jellabas, *gandoras* (men's embroidered jacket and pants) and *jabadors* (men's garment which is worn under a jellaba), both

machine- and hand-embroidered. There's a fountain in this souk, as well as in the next one, **Souk Selham**. Here a good-quality *burnous* (hooded cape for men) made of the finest wool costs Dh600. Other shops sell haberdashery. The last of these souks is **L'Bali**. This souk used to sell old clothes, but now sells lengths of cloth (for women at around Dh200) for jellabas, and *babouches* (leather slippers); for the latter, check out Alami Hassan (p51).

### ☑ BAB BOU JELOUD
**northwestern medina**
Everyone comes through this main gate at some point during their stay as it leads to a clutch of restaurants and the main shopping streets. Decorated with blue *zellij* on the outside and green on the inside, it's relatively young — only 200 years old. The **Tourist Police Brigade** has its headquarters here.

### ☑ BAB GUISSA
**northern medina**
This gate was built in the 12th century. A bird market is held here on Friday mornings, outside the walls. Just inside the gate is a square with a large fountain, the Bab Guissa mosque and the *medersa* which is still in use today. The air is scented with cedarwood from the large number of carpentry workshops in the area.

Courtyard and gardens of the Batha Museum

## ☺ BATHA
**Pl de l'Independence; western medina**
Its real name is Pl de
l'Independence but it's generally
called 'Batha' and is one of the
main entrances to the medina,
with parking and taxis. On the
square are Café Firdaous (p69)
and La Maison Bleue (p59), as well
as **Dar Mekaour**, where Morocco's
Independence Manifesto was
signed in 1944.

## ☺ BATHA MUSEUM
**Rue de la Musée, Batha; admission Dh10;
⟳ 8.30am-4.30pm Wed-Mon**
This building, Sultan Moulay
Abd al-Aziz's summer palace,

was completed at the end of the
19th century. Converted into a
museum in 1916, it houses mostly
18th-century Fassi items, including
musical instruments, embroidery,
clothing and jewellery, as well
as carpets from the Middle Atlas
Berber tribes. Of note is the 10th-
century *minbar* (pulpit) from the
Al-Andalous Mosque (p84). The
signage describing the artefacts
is in French and Arabic. Across
the garden, the rest of the palace
is closed, except for a tiny room
where a man produces boxes,
letter openers and trinkets in
fine wood-marquetry, just as he
has for 50 years. The garden has

been lovingly restored by ADER (Agency for the Dedensification & Rehabilitation of the Fez Medina) based on the original plans. It contains a venerable holm oak that has grown much bigger than these trees usually do – perhaps especially for the artists who perform in its shade at the afternoon concerts of the Fes Festival of World Sacred Music (p12).

## ☉ BELGHAZI MUSEUM
☎ 035 741178; 19 Derb Ghorba, Guerniz; admission Dh40;
🕑 9am-6.30pm

This private museum is housed in a magnificent riad with a shady tea garden in the courtyard. The four main salons have jewellery, weapons and embroidery, and smaller rooms contain writing implements, manuscripts and musical instruments. Upstairs there's a gallery selling similar pieces, and to top it off there's a roof terrace with excellent views of the medina.

## ☉ BLACKSMITH
Haddadine, off Talaa Kebira, Ain Allou;
🕑 8am-noon & 3-6pm Sat-Thu

One of the last blacksmiths working in the traditional way, Tayeb el-Mendri fashions wrought-iron window screens and balcony inserts in curly arabesque designs using a coal fire, bellows and an anvil.

## ☉ BOU INANIA MEDERSA
Talaa Kebira; admission Dh10;
🕑 9am-6pm, closed at prayer times

Built between 1350 and 1356, this *medersa* is one of the most important sights in Fez. It was restored a few years ago. Inside the massive carved brass doors is a restful marble-floored space with central fountain, carved cedarwood *mashrabiya* panels screening the students' cells, very fine *zellij* and intricately carved plaster. Look out for the *mihrab* (niche indicating direction of Mecca) with its beautiful ceiling and the onyx marble

## WRITTEN IN STONE
Arabic calligraphy is an art form whose patterns symbolise the infinite creation of Allah. Used not only for writing and for copying the Quran, it's also found carved on walls and columns in *medersas* (theological colleges) and mosques. Kufi script is the heavy, black angular writing that is sometimes ornamented with leaves and flowers. The more flowing cursive script found on buildings is called Thuluth and was developed in the 13th century. In the Fez *medersas* there are good examples of both scripts, carved into *zellij* (mosaic tilework), in plaster and on marble columns. Sometimes ceilings and walls are adorned with painted Andalusi script, a flowing style adorned with flowers and leaves.

columns. The *medersa* is unusual in that it also has a mosque with a particularly beautiful minaret covered in green *zellij*. This is best viewed from east of the *medersa*, or from the terrace of Café Clock (p64).

### CHEMMAINE SOUK

Near the Kairaouine Mosque, this was once the place to buy candles. It's now resplendent with colourful embroidered velvet outfits for weddings and circumcisions, wedding chairs, fezzes and, curiously, lots of dried-fruit and nut stalls. The Chemmaine Funduq is

Pyramids of dried-fruit and nuts, Chemmaine Souk

in bad disrepair and is not open to the public.

### CHOUWARA TANNERIES
**Derb Chouwara, Blida**

In this, the largest of the tanneries, workers treat, scrape and dye animal skins in a series of pits. The dyes are mostly made of plants such an indigo and poppies. A walk along Derb Chouwara will result in numerous invitations, from shop-owners and their touts, to terraces where you'll get a good view of the pits. Mint leaves ward off the smell!

### CHRABLIYINE MOSQUE
**Talaa Kebira**

This must certainly be the prettiest minaret in town. Around the mosque there is a fountain, a *medersa* with good *mashrabiya* (intricate carved wood) panels at street level and windows above the street, and an ablution facility. Chrabliyine means 'the street of the slipper-makers'.

### DAR ADIYEL
**Oued Rchacha, Derb Sidi Nalli, Guerniz; admission Dh10;** 9am-1pm Mon-Fri, 9am-1pm & 2.30-6pm Sat & Sun

The wealthy Adiyel family were merchants who held top government posts, and this impressive 18th-century house belonged to Abdelkhaleq Adiyel, the governor

Working a hide with saffron dye at the tanneries

of Fez. Restored in 1993 with funds from the Italian government, it is now a conservatory for Moroccan-Andalusian music. Students give concerts at 3pm Monday to Thursday at no extra charge.

### ◎ DAR BA MOHAMED BEN CHERGUI
**Derb el-Horra;** 🕙 **9am-6pm**
This magnificent place belonged to a previous pasha of Fez, Ba Mohamed ben Chergui. There are two houses in the complex – one

the main house for the men, the other the harem. The harem has a remarkable garden made of raised star shaped flower beds. Inside, the hammam is worth a visit, and look out for the black-and-white photograph of the last pasha to live there. It's all decaying badly, though the complex is up for sale. The caretaker is happy to show people around the ground floor of the main house, the hammam, and the harem garden. Tip him about Dh20.

## DAR GLAOUI

**☎ 067 366828; 1 Derb el-Hamiya, Ziat**

Probably the most impressive residence in Fez, this 150-year-old palace comprises some 17 houses, stables, a mausoleum and cemetery, Quranic school, hammam, garages and two large gardens. It's privately owned by the El-Glaoui family of Marrakesh, but you can make an appointment to view it with Abdou (phone after midday). Abdou, whose art is on display at the entrance, will show you the massive courtyard and four salons resplendent with carved, painted wood, carved plaster, Iraqi glass and carved and painted 'stalactites'. He will also take you to the kitchen (large enough to serve the entire complex), which leads to the harem, with another courtyard, wall fountain and dilapidated painted wood balconies. It is all in dire need of repair, but it's for sale – €10 million and it's yours – though it might well cost several times that amount to renovate. Abdou appreciates a tip (per person about Dh20).

## DAR PACHA TAZI

**Sidi el-Khayat, Batha**

Set within a large garden with trellis-covered walkways, this 20th-century palace has housed various government figures. It's now the headquarters of the Fès Saïss Association that organises

the Fes Festival of World Sacred Music (p12).

## DEMNATI FOUNTAIN & DAR DMANA

**Derb Jamaa el-Hamiya, Chrabliyine**

This street opens out into a square with an ancient mulberry tree. There's an exceptionally tall traditional house, Dar Dmana, with a massive studded door, and the Demnati fountain. Wait a while, and you might see magnificent stallions being washed, their manes and tails stained red with henna. Also here is an antique shop worth a browse, Brocante Bab Touta (p53).

## DIWANE MOSQUE

**Derb Diwane, Sagha**

It's worth taking a look at this mosque (even though you can't go inside unless you're a Muslim). The door and its canopy are beautiful examples of carved, painted wood, and there's carved plaster too.

## EL-MAKOUDI MOSQUE

**Derb el-Makoudi, Lihoudi**

This mosque is in the formerly Jewish area of Lihoudi (p47), and is one of the few that doesn't have a minaret. The mosque's fountain is at the top of the street, and is particularly beautiful with carved *medluk* (fine sand-and-lime coating) and intricate *zellij*.

### ◙ FUNDUQ KAAT SMEN
**off Talaa Kebira, Derraqine;** ⏰ **8am-8pm Sat-Thu**

Shops here are devoted to the sale of *smen* (rancid butter), olive oil, *khlia* (preserved meat) and honey. **Chez Nafis Chergui** has wild rosemary, orange flower or eucalyptus honey, argan oil (produced from the fruit of the argan tree) and olive oil. There are a couple of carpet shops at the entrance to the *funduq*.

### ◙ FUNDUQ TASTAWNIYINE
**Derb Boutouil**

This *funduq* housed merchants coming from Tetouan to do business in Fez. It still has some intricate *mashrabiya* on the upper

balconies but, like all the *funduqs*, it's in bad repair. Today you'll find a carpet shop and a carpenter in residence.

### ◙ FUNDUQ TAZI
**Talaa Kebira, Derraqine**

Opposite Funduq Kaat Smen (left), Funduq Tazi has a leather shop, Maison D'Artisanat (p59), and some drum-makers who use the skins for their ceramic *tam-tams* (drums). It's a simple building with no decorative elements.

### ◙ HENNA SOUK
**Derb Fakharine**

One of the oldest market places this souk, off Talaa Kebira, has graceful plane trees shading

Hunt for treasure at the Henna Souk

the stalls selling ceramics and traditional cosmetics, including henna. The *mohtassib* (price-controller), now defunct, had his office here and you can still see his large scales. On one side is the restored **Maristane Sidi Frej**, a former psychiatric hospital built by the Merinids in the 13th century. Leo

Africanus (p122) worked here as a young man. It's now a small *kis-saria* (covered market).

###  KAIRAOUINE LIBRARY
**Seffarine Sq**

This has always been a reference library, and valuable books such as those by Averroes and Ibn Khaldun

Open door to prayer and learning at the Kairaouine Mosque & University

have survived. The reading room was built in 1940 and the building is well restored.

### ◎ KAIRAOUINE MOSQUE & UNIVERSITY
**central medina**

The largest mosque in Africa, the Kairaouine claims to be the oldest university in the world. A wide variety of subjects was taught here, which is why Fez became such a centre of learning, culture and religious tolerance. Currently undergoing restoration, the mosque should have re-opened (to Muslims only) early in 2008. The complex has grown since its founding In 859 and has many beautiful elements such as the pavilions, *mihrab* and decorative plasterwork, cedarwood and *zellij* reminiscent of the Alhambra in Spain. It has a 10th-century square minaret with cupola. The mosque was expanded to its current size under the Almoravids in the 12th century. Surrounding it are several *medersas*.

### ◎ LIHOUDI
**south of Bab Guissa**

This neighbourhood is bordered by Derb Funduq Lihoudi, Derb Makoudi, Achebine and Haffarine. It once had a large Jewish population, most of them jewellers. Run down today, it was once a wealthy area. On Derb Funduq Lihoudi, etched into a wall over the street, is a Star of David inside an eight-pointed star demarcating the Jewish area.

### ◎ L'MARQTANE
**Achebine, Sagha; ◉ 9am–noon**

Follow a dark passage into this enclosed square north of Sagha and imagine being sold: this used to be an old slave market. Now it's a secondhand clothing market in the mornings (hugely crowded at weekends). A good search can turn up superb antique velvet

---

### SACRED GEOMETRY

Everywhere you look are geometric shapes in *zellij* (mosaic tilework), sculpted plaster and painted wood. Stand and stare for a while and fall into a contemplation on the patterns that seem to have no beginning and no end. *Zellij* stars can have 48, 64 and even 96 points and display magnificent craftsmanship based on the number forms and rhythms of ancient Greek mathematicians such as Pythagoras and Euclid.

Squares indicate the four elements as well as the base of the Kaaba in Mecca; triangles are based on earth and point to heaven; circles represent the infinite, the eight-pointed star the seal of Solomon, and spirals the labyrinth through which initiates of mystical and religious philosophies must pass.

caftans rich with silver embroidery, or a silk *takshita* (garment worn over a caftan) for weddings.

### ◎ MERENID TOMBS
**north of the medina**
These 14th-century tombs are in ruins now, but command a good view over the city and the ramparts, as well as to the Borj Sud in the south and the rolling hills to the north. Take a taxi to the tombs (from Batha Dh7) and avoid the quasi guides. Walk back down the goat paths to the main road (look out for the caves where people still live). Once across the road, turn left for Bab Guissa or right for Ain Azleten – the walk back to the medina takes around 10 minutes.

### ◎ MOKRI PALACE
**Chaq Bdenjala, Ziat;** ☽ **9am-7pm**
For a modest tip, Azzedine will show you around the large rectangular courtyard with salons at each end. Upstairs are gracious rooms, the venue for concerts (see p72), looking over the medina. The palace is up for sale, and is likely to be turned into a luxury hotel.

### ◎ MOULAY IDRISS MZARA
**btwn Derb el-Horra & Funduq Tazi, Talaa Kebira**
This ancient niche in the wall is covered in *zellij* and surrounded by carved plaster. Rather than go

all the way down to Moulay Idriss Zawiya, devotees can venerate their saint here.

### ◎ MOULAY IDRISS ZAWIYA
Here is the heart of Fez: the mausoleum of the city's founder and the most venerated pilgrimage spot in Morocco. You can't enter unless you're a Muslim, but you can peek inside. It's worth walking around the building to see the beautiful carved and painted wood porches, the wall *zellij* and painted carved plaster at each doorway. Near the main entrance are a fountain and a *mzara* (niche on the outside wall, richly decorated with *zellij* and plasterwork) where people in too much of a hurry to enter can pay their respects; there's another *mzara* on Talaa Kebira (left). The brass money-slot is for giving alms. Housing a mosque and ablution facilities, as well as the tomb of Moulay Idriss, the *zawiya* (shrine) dates from the 9th century and was enlarged in the 17th century. The streets around the *zawiya* sell necessities for pilgrims: votive candles, prayer beads and various types of incense.

### ◎ NEJJARINE SQUARE
The interesting Nejjarine Sq is dominated by the beautifully restored **Nejjarine Wood Museum** (admission Dh20; ☽ 10am-7pm), housed

in an 18th-century *funduq*. There's also a superbly decorated wall fountain. Pause a while in a café or browse the shops before venturing into the carpenters' souk with its amazing array of glitzy wedding chairs.

### ◎ QBIEB NAQES
**Sagha**

This little street is full of food stands. The *qbieb* (water conduit) itself is the small arched fountain at this crossroads in the middle of Sagha. Undecorated and seemingly insignificant, it was the main water conduit for this area and therefore an important element of daily life.

### ◎ RIYAD MOKRI
**Oued Souaffine, Ziat;** 🕑 **8am-6.30pm**

This fabulous house, formerly owned by the powerful Mokri family, is now home to the Institute of Traditional Building Crafts. Students learn carpentry, wood painting, plaster sculpture

and design. The house is surely an inspiration to them with its carved and painted doors, spectacular ceilings and wonderful views. The gardens are the best in Fez, full of fruit trees, jasmine, honeysuckle, rosemary, lavender and plumbago. Do tip the person who shows you around (about Dh20).

### ◎ SAGHA SQUARE
**Sagha**

This square contains the 18th-century **Sagha Funduq** with magnificent *mashrabiya* panels. The scales in the courtyard were for weighing fleeces; cotton and wool are still sold here. Near the entrance is a fountain with a tiled *koubba* (dome-shaped roof). There's also the fascinating Café Ba Bouchta (p69) opposite the *funduq*.

### ◎ SEFFARINE MEDERSA
**Seffarine Sq; admission Dh10;** 🕑 **9am-6pm, closed at prayer times**

Built in 1270 and still in use today, this is the oldest of the Merinid

---

**WORTH THE TRIP**

For an overview of the city and great photo opportunities, take a petit taxi round the ramparts (two hours Dh200). Driving up through the cemeteries west of the bus station, turn right at the top to the Borj Nord (Northern Fortress). The building has been restored as an **armaments museum** (admission Dh10; 🕑 8.30am-6pm Tue-Sun). The city walls are being repaired according to traditional building techniques at a cost of Dh35 million. Continue round to the Borj Sud (Southern Fortress) for a superb view of the medina. Both fortresses were built by the Saadians, as much to keep the locals in check as to keep Fez safe from marauding Berber tribes.

Time is fluid at the Water Clock, on Talaa Kebira

*medersas* in Fez. The prayer hall contains what's thought to be the oldest *mihrab* in the city. It has a minaret with colourful *zellij*. There's a rectangular pool in the central courtyard.

### ◉ SEFFARINE SQUARE

Here's a delightful square to rest a while under the plane tree and soak up the atmosphere of the medina. On one side lies the Kairaouine Library; on the other, the Seffarine Medersa (p49), and all around are coppersmiths hammering their wares into shape: huge cauldrons, stills for making rosewater, kettles, pots and samovars.

### ◉ SIDI AHMED TIJANI ZAWIYA
**Derb Rhabt l'Qaïs, Blida**
The resting place of the founder of the Tariqa Tijaniya, a Sufi brotherhood, this exquisite *zawiya* and mosque is of great importance to devotees from all over North and West Africa, who visit it on their way to Mecca. It's greatly revered in Fez, second only to the Moulay Idriss Zawiya.

### ◉ WATER CLOCK
**Talaa Kebira**
Opposite the Bou Inania Medersa entrance, there are 12 windows above 13 carved beams sticking out of the wall. It's said brass bowls were set on the beams

and that water flowed into them, making them chime out the hours of prayer. No-one knows how it worked; its secret lies buried with the magician who invented it.

# 🛍 SHOP

The main shopping streets are Talaa Kebira and Talaa Seghira, but it's worth getting lost to find little shops tucked away down side streets and in squares. Fez is a shopaholic's delight: look for leather, the famous blue-glazed ceramics, lamps, jewellery, carpets, antiques and brassware. See p127 for information on business hours.

## 🏠 ABDALLAH OUAZZANI IBRAHIMI
*Carpets, Textiles & Embroidery*
☎ 035 635934; 84 Talaa Kebira, Chrabli-yine; ⏱ 9am-6pm, closed Fri prayers
There are two rooms in this shop; one sells the usual range of carpets, while the other has interesting old hand-embroidered caftans and jellabas from around Dh300. A thick woollen jellaba costs Dh500 and a *burnous* Dh400.

## 🏠 ALAMI HASSAN *Slippers*
☎ 035 638094; Souk L'Bali, Attarine, Talaa Kebira; ⏱ 9am-8pm Sat-Thu
Every colour and style of *babouche* you can think of is displayed in the otherwise rather drab Souk L'Bali. They range from Dh50 a pair up to

Dh200 for the best quality; red or yellow round toed Berber slippers for men go for Dh80 to Dh150.

## 🏠 ALLAL ART GALLERY
*Art & Antiques*
☎ 035 635144; 74 bis Derb Rhabt l'Qaïs, Blida; ⏱ 8.30am-7.30pm
This Aladdin's cave stocks a wide range of pierced-metal lamps and light fittings, wooden doors and windows, *mashrabiya* panels and jewellery.

## 🏠 ANTIQUITÉ NEJJARINE
*Antiques*
☎ 060 539224; 3 Nejjarine Sq; ⏱ 10am-7pm Sat-Thu
Samir Bousfiha's shop bulges with antiques – large pieces of furniture, doors and even whole painted ceilings, as well as smaller items such as wooden writing boards at around Dh1000 for an original, or Dh600 for a copy. For more portable souvenirs, check out the wide range of silver jewellery: thick bangles, old *fibulas* (brooches) and necklaces. Old silver is Dh15 per gram.

## 🏠 ART DU BRONZE *Metalwork*
☎ 035 740277; www.artdubronze.ma; 35 Talaa Seghira; ⏱ 9am-7pm
Handcrafted brass and metalware gleam from every corner of this large shop. Much is made on the premises and you can see the

Heavy metal: craftsman at work at Art Du Bronze (p51)

craftsman at work every day from 9am to 5pm. Brass plates and tea-pots start at around Dh150. Good quality camel-bone mirrors start at Dh500 and there are filigree lanterns from around Dh2500.

### ◨ AU COIN DU BOIS
*Antiques & Woodwork*
☎ 035 636732; 20 Derb el-Hammam, Guerniz; ⌚ 9am-7pm

Worth visiting if only to see a beautiful example of a Fassi house, this shop stocks large pieces of furniture which they'll arrange to ship home for you. There are tables, doors and windows, cup-boards and chairs – some antique and some not. An old carved door

will set you back some Dh4500, a carved and painted box Dh1700.

### ◨ AU PETIT BAZAR DU BON ACCEUIL *Antiques & Jewellery*
☎ 035 633764; 35 Talaa Seghira; ⌚ 9am-8pm Sat-Thu, closed noon-2pm Fri

This treasure-house is worth a visit. It stocks old and modern jewellery including some seriously good Berber pieces such as *fibulas* and pendants, old carpets and traditional clothing, *objets d'art*, embroidery, ceramics, glassware and metalware. Upstairs are good pieces of wooden furniture. Women by themselves may not feel comfortable shopping here.

## 🄾 BACHIR EL-MESKI *Leather*
☎ 035 637162; 50 Talaa Kebira, Ras Tayaline; 🕑 8am-8pm Sat-Thu
Coin purses, wallets and handbags in all colours abound in this shop (from Dh5). Sandals and round-toed Berber slippers cost Dh30 to Dh100. There are pouffes from Dh55 to Dh300: goatskin is at the upper end of this price range, while tooled camel- and goatskin is Dh150.

## 🄾 BASKET SHOP
*Traditional Craft*
72 Talaa Kebira, Ras Tayaline; 🕑 9am-6pm Sat-Thu
Ba Hamid sells round wooden sieves starting at Dh7 and place mats at Dh10. He has a wide range of baskets, including conical-lidded breadbaskets (from Dh40 to Dh110 depending on size), and this is the place to get your *couscoussier* (the pot in which couscous is steamed) for Dh70.

## 🄾 BRASSWARE SHOP
*Metalwork*
59 Talaa Kebira, Qantrat Bourous; 🕑 8.30am-7pm Sat-Thu
There are several small metalwork shops in this area. Ali Benjelloun has some good Hand of Fatima doorknockers in the shape of a hand (Dh80), as well as a flat stylised version (Dh100). There's another **shop** (54 Talaa Kebira) that has

shiny silver-plated teapots (Dh180), and orange flower water shakers and incense burners (both Dh70).

## 🄾 BROCANTE BAB TOUTA
*Antiques*
☎ 061 796515; 18 Seqqaït Demnati, Ain Azleten; 🕑 9am-7pm Sat-Thu
Squeeze into Abderrahim's tiny shop crammed with old teapots, zany photos, fabrics, carpets and larger pieces of furniture. It's worth a browse in this delightful small square (see p44) with its fountain and ancient mulberry tree.

## 🄾 BUCKET MAKER
*Traditional Craft*
Talaa Kebira, Chrabliyine; 🕑 9am-noon Sat-Thu, closed in Aug
Sidi Tazi is the last bucket-maker in Fez and his wares are sought-after all over the country. The cedarwood buckets (depending on size from Dh70 to Dh150) are for use in the hammam.

## 🄾 CARD SHOP *Art*
114 Talaa Kebira; 🕑 9.30am-7pm Sat-Thu
This pretty little shop sells good-quality postcards (Dh2), cards featuring scenes of Fez with envelopes (Dh7) and posters that range from Dh35 to Dh90. There are some gifts too such as *tadelakt* (smooth, lustrous lime plaster) lamps at Dh150.

### Si Mohammed el-Amrani
*Herbalist, Coin de Henne*

**Best-selling line** Ras el-hanoot (shopkeeper's spice mixture), a blend of 19 spices used in Moroccan cooking. The best quality costs Dh40 for 100g. **What women want** A remedy for falling hair: a mix of grapeseed, avocado and argan oils with black seed (Nigella sativa), known locally as 'seeds of blessing'. **What men want** An aphrodisiac that apparently puts store-bought ones to shame: 20 ingredients, including ginseng and anise, mixed with honey. **What's best for stomach problems?** Dried pomegranate skin ground with medicinal herbs and mixed with honey. **Where does the knowledge come from?** It's passed on from an ancient friend and I have lot of books, but there's no formal training in herbalism in Morocco. **Where are the snakeskins, chameleons and tortoises that you see in other herbalist shops?** Those are just for magic potions that don't work – I'm interested in the medicinal use of herbs.
*Interview by Helen Ranger*

## 🏠 CHEZ BOUTBI NADIA
*Ceramics*

☎ 070 853785; 14 Talaa Kebira;
🕐 8am-9pm Sat-Thu

Nadia is one of the few women shopkeepers in the medina. Her small shop sells traditional Fassi ceramics at excellent prices (tiny tajines for salt and pepper Dh15; plates from Dh35) and it's the best place for that tajine so you can cook Moroccan-style at home (tajine for three servings Dh40, for six servings Dh50).

## 🏠 CHEZ LA FAMILLE BERBÈRE
*Metalwork & Ceramics*

☎ 035 741229; 27 Ras Tayaline;
🕐 9am-8pm

Khalid and Zouhaïr pride themselves on their metalwork lamps; a wall sconce in wrought iron and copper is Dh60. They also have a wide range of ceramics, small pieces of wooden furniture (a collapsible carved cedarwood table inlaid with brass is Dh600) and decorated tea glasses (each Dh10). This place is off Talaa Kebira.

## 🏠 COIN BERBERE
*Antiques, Carpets & Jewellery*

☎ 035 636946; bouzidi8000@hotmail
.com; 67 Talaa Kebira, Haddadine;
🕐 10am-8pm

A trio of shops can be found here at the junction of Talaa Kebira and Derb el-Horra, all owned by the Bouzidi-Idrissi family. The largest stocks seriously good antique ceramics, embroidery, doors and furniture. Across the street is a carpet shop with antique and new carpets made by various Berber tribes, and next door to that is good jewellery, mostly silver and coral.

## 🏠 COIN DE HENNE
*Perfumes & Incense, Herbs & Spices*

☎ 035 740555; 22/23 Talaa Kebira,
Haddadine, Ain Allou; 🕐 10am-8pm
Sat-Thu

This tiny shop stocks medicinal herbs and spices, essential oils, flower waters and perfumes. Si Mohammed el Amrani sells good honey from the south (250g for Dh75), and tubs of argan oil–based cream for wrinkles. There's also traditional incense, including gum arabic, sandalwood and frankincense. And wonderful clocks!

## 🏠 COIN DES INSTRUMENTS
## MUSICAL *Musical Instruments*

☎ 035 638232; music_himdi@hotmail
.com; 51 Derb Fakharine; 🕐 9am-9pm
Sat-Thu

Ahmed stocks both decorative and professional musical instruments. A good *oud* (lute) will set you back around Dh1500 to Dh2000; a ceramic *darbuka* (goblet drum) is Dh400; a *hadjouj* (bass lute) around Dh400 and a *gimbri* (a type of lute) between Dh50 and Dh300, depending on size. A pair of *garagab* (Gnaoua metal castanets) goes for Dh50 to Dh100.

### 🖰 COOPERATIVE ARTISANALE (LEATHERWORKER'S COOPERATIVE) *Leather*
**Cooperative Artisanale des Patrons Maroquiniers de Fes; ☎ 035 633213; 42 Talaa Kebira, Ain Allou; 🕙 10am-8pm Sat-Thu**

Just about anything made of leather can be found in this shop, with the exception of clothing. A large portmanteau is Dh400, a briefcase around Dh200, handbags are Dh120 and you can expect to pay around Dh260 for an embroidered pouffe. Put a hat on your head for Dh60.

### 🖰 CURIOSITES BERBERES *Carpets*
**☎ 035 635569; 33 Zqaq Lehjar, Talaa Seghira; 🕙 9am-8pm**

Here's a wide range of kilims and carpets from various Berber tribes. A 1.60m x 1.20m rug woven from aloe silk in jewel-like colours is Dh420; a large *hendira* (traditional woven cloak) with thick loops on the back is Dh4000 and a 2.5m x 3m rustic red Chichoua carpet with Berber designs costs around Dh5000.

### 🖰 DRIED FRUIT SHOP *Food & Drink*
**Chemmaine Sq; 🕙 8am-8pm Sat-Thu**

Hafid Alaoui sits plum in the middle of his meticulous pyramids of dried fruit and nuts at this large stall next to the Chemmaine Funduq. The very best quality dates come from Erfoud (per kilogram Dh150). There are also apricots (per kilogram Dh60), plump almonds (per kilogram Dh120) and pecan nuts in the shell (per kilogram Dh100).

### 🖰 ECH CHAHED YOUSSEF *Ceramics*
**☎ 067 695006; 12 Talaa Kebira, Derraqine; 🕙 9.30am-8pm Sat-Thu**

Youssef's small shop stocks ceramics and some lamps. An old platter costs around Dh350 and a new reproduction Dh200. Cheer up your bathroom with a Fassi-style painted ceramic basin at Dh300. Candlesticks are Dh50. He also makes to order.

### 🖰 FÈS ART GALLERY *Antiques*
**☎ 035 634663; 2 Derb Boutouil; 🕙 8.30am-7pm**

The management can be somewhat snooty, but the furniture and *objets d'art* are worth a look. There are exquisite inlaid chairs, tables and cupboards from Syria, some reasonable paintings and ceramics, and good jewellery. From the

Kilim time at carpet specialists Curiosites Berberes

roof terrace the view over the Kairaouine is excellent.

### ☐ GALERIE JAMIL DES BEAUX ARTS *Art*

☎ 035 740207; galeriejamil-a-p-fes@caramail.com; 11 Sbetriyine, Seffarine; ☽ 10am-8pm Mon-Thu & Sat, 10am-noon Fri

While art on the street is naïf at best, this gallery just off Seffarine Sq offers interesting work, mostly in oils, by Fassi father-and-son team Hassan and Mohammed Jamil. Other artists are represented too, and there are *objets d'art* such as painted doors on sale.

### ☐ GALERIE NEJARINE

*Ceramics, Leather & Woodwork*
☎ 035 633581; ahmedartisanal@hotmail.com; 15 Talaa Kebira, Ain Allou; ☽ 8.30am-8pm Sat-Thu, 8.30am-12.30pm Fri

Ahmed specialises in reproductions of old ceramics: while a 10-year-old bowl in his shop costs around Dh650, reproductions are Dh250. He also has small bowls (Dh25), resin and bronze candleholders (depending on size Dh150 to Dh750), and two-seater rectangular pouffes (Dh400). He's contracted to **Medina Express** ( ☎ 082 006060) so shipping things home is safe and easy.

## ◻ GHAZAL MILOUD
*Food & Drink*

☎ 035 638780; 205 Talaa Kebira;
🕑 8am-9pm, closed at prayer times

Every type of olive can be found here, along with preserved lemons and various vegetables that gleam colourfully from the shelves. Olives flavoured with chillies or lemon rind cost Dh16 per kilogram.

## ◻ HERBORISTERIE BOU INANIA
*Perfumes & Incense, Herbs & Spices*

☎ 035 638760; Derb Moulay Abdellma-lik; 🕑 9.30am-7.30pm

This large shop sells natural soaps (best-quality argan Dh40), vegetable oils such as argan and olive, essential oils, musk perfume, *ghassoul* (clay that comes in chips or powder form) which is a natural soap and exfoliant excellent for skin and hair, and incense. There's also a wide range of traditional medicines and spices (1g saffron Dh10). It's off Talaa Kebira, near the Bou Inania Medersa.

## ◻ KELIM BERBER *Carpets*
035 636351; 37 Zqaq el-Maa, Chrabliyine;
🕑 9am-6pm Sat-Thu,9am-noon Fri

Here's a large shop, of Talaa Kebira, with a wide range of old and new carpets, *hendiras* and cushion covers. A thick, creamy new Beni Ouaraine carpet measuring 3m x 2m costs Dh1500, whereas an old one is Dh6000. A bright red 2m x 1m Zemmor kilim with Berber patterns is Dh900; an old 2.5m x 1.80m Zaiane carpet is Dh4500. Cushion covers range from Dh40 to Dh600.

## ◻ KISSARIAT *Slippers*
Talaa Kebira; 🕑 9am-noon & 3-8pm, closed Fri afternoons

The *kissariat* (covered markets) at the bottom of Talaa Kebira have dozens of tiny shops selling *babouches* in every colour, fabric and design. A top-quality, hand-stitched pair of leather *babouches* costs around Dh120. Only men wear yellow or white. Venture further into the *kissariat* to discover a wealth of bright yellow-gold wedding jewellery and superb fabrics.

## ◻ L'ART BLEU
*Textiles & Embroidery*

☎ 035 636486; 1bis Hay Lablida, Derb el-Alami, Blida; 🕑 8am-8pm

A glorious profusion of colour greets you in this shop of silk fabrics made from aloe cactus. There are scarves (Dh80) and bed covers (3m x 2m Dh300, 3m x 2.5m Dh400, 3m x 3m Dh500). Ali will make them to order on the looms in the shop with one day's notice; just choose your colours.

## GET AHEAD – GET A FEZ

Worn by cartoon monkeys in hammocks, by languorous men in smoking jackets or by the late British comedian Tommy Cooper, the fez has always been seen as a bit of exotica. It's Turkish, but was banned by Atatürk in 1925. It's seen service as a military cap in several countries. Crafted in Fez to this day, it's now only worn by elderly men or for celebrations such as weddings and circumcisions. Designed as a head covering to be worn during prayer (with no brim the forehead can touch the ground), the fez is made of red felt and has a black tassel. You can buy one in the souks around Moulay Idriss Zawiya for about Dh20.

### ☐ L'ART TRADITIONNEL
*Metalwork & Woodwork*
☎ 035 635769; 8 Derb Boutouil;
🕙 9am-8pm Sat-Thu, 9am-noon Fri

Pierced brass, sometimes with opaque or coloured Iraqi glass, is used for all the lanterns here: an ostrich-egg size costs Dh900, a small lantern Dh1400 and one with glass inserts Dh1200. There are also carved wooden chests (around Dh1700), tables and old doors. The shop is contracted to **Medina Express** ( ☎ 082 006060) for easy shipping.

### ☐ MAISON BLEUE *Ceramics*
☎ 064 056857; Zqaq Lehjar, 68 Talaa Seghira; 🕙 9am-9pm

It's worth visiting this shop just to see the magnificent small house it's in, complete with balconies, painted ceilings and intricate plasterwork, occupied by the family who run the place. There's a veritable treasure trove of plates, dishes, bowls and more in the traditional designs of Fez.

Plates cost from Dh200, soap dishes are Dh40 and small bowls Dh30.

### ☐ MAISON D'ARTISANAT
*Leather*
☎ 035 634436; Funduq Tazi, Talaa Kebira; 🕙 9am-7pm Sat-Thu

Here you can find pouffes, shoes, bags and belts at reasonable prices, all made right here in the Funduq Tazi (p45).

### ☐ MAISON DES BRODEUSES
**FASSIES** *Textiles & Embroidery*
☎ 035 741942; 29 Derb Bine Lamssari, Guerniz; 🕙 9am-7pm

You can watch women using embroidery hoops here, working on a good-quality cotton-linen mix. Mostly it's traditional Fassi blue embroidery on white cloth. Placemats cost from Dh100 each, depending on the amount of work involved, and a 2.5m x 1.5m tablecloth with 12 serviettes costs Dh400.

## BERBER JEWELLERY

Berber jewellery is made of silver. A girl collects it from childhood and receives a great deal on her marriage. For weddings and *moussems* (pilgrimages or festivals) Berber women wear head ornaments with dangling coins, earrings so large they're supported by a chain over the head, pendants on the forehead, necklaces, rings, bracelets and anklets, and *fibulas* (brooches to hold scarves and cloaks in place). The heavy silver is decorated with niello work (a black metallic inlay), enamel, engraving, and semiprecious stones. Coral and amber are popular beads. By the Prophet's example, men wear no jewellery except a silver wedding ring and, these days, a watch.

### MAISON SAHARA
*Ceramics & Woodwork*
☎ 065 735681; 9 Nejjarine Sq; 🕑 9am-7.30pm Sat-Thu
Berber and Riffian pots abound in this shop, some ancient and some copies. An old pot might cost Dh250 while a copy is about Dh130. There are also old wedding chests from the Rif in northwest Morocco (around Dh2000) and painted cedarwood boxes from Dh750.

### MAT MAKER
*Traditional Craft*
Derb Jammala; 🕑 9am-7pm Sat-Thu
The last craftsman left making dried grass mats by hand, Saïd

Laghzaoui is worth visiting to see this dying craft. The mats are used in mosques, but you can also buy placemats (each Dh10). It's off Talaa Kebira.

### MISTER CUIR MAROCAIN
*Leather*
☎ 068 353742; 1 Zqaq Lehjar, Talaa Seghira; 🕑 9am-7pm
There's a wide range of leather jackets and coats in this shop; black and dark brown are cheaper than tan and other colours. Men's jackets are around Dh800; women's jackets Dh650, or Dh 750 for a three-quarter length jacket.

### NAJIB CUIR *Leather*
120 Talaa Kebira, Chrabliyine; 🕑 10am-6pm Sat-Thu
This small shop sells sandals (Dh30 to Dh100), belts (from Dh30), handbags and satchels (from Dh150) and briefcases (a good-quality one at Dh350).

### NEQ BRODERIE
*Textiles & Embroidery*
☎ 035 636294; neqbroderie@yahoo.fr; 67 Derb Rahba; 🕑 9am-7pm Sat-Thu, closed Fri afternoons
Walk right to the end of this grubby lane, off Talaa Kebira near the Bou Inania Medersa, and into a modern-looking house (signposted from Talaa Kebira). It's worth the effort: here is

handcrafted traditional Fassi embroidery (watch the women at work) on excellent quality cotton-linen mix. Placemats cost Dh100 to Dh200; a tablecloth and six napkins from Dh450; napkins are Dh70 each.

### 🛍 NOUGAT SHOP
*Food & Drink*
**Bab Moulay Idriss, Nejjarine;** 🕐 **8am-8pm Sat-Thu**
All around the Kairaouine and Moulay Idriss Zawiya are nougat shops and stalls with pink, white and green slabs of nut-studded nougat, all buzzing with bees. The slabs at this little shop are Dh15 per kilogram, or you can try a small basket of mixed nougats (Dh3) or a medium-sized one (Dh10).

### 🛍 PARFUMERIE MEDINA
*Perfumes & Incense*
☎ **035 630609; 7 Henna Souk;** 🕐 **9am-7pm**
The knowledgeable owner Rachid Ouedrhiri will explain all about the perfumes, cosmetics and es-sential oils he stocks in his small stall in the Henna Souk (p45), off

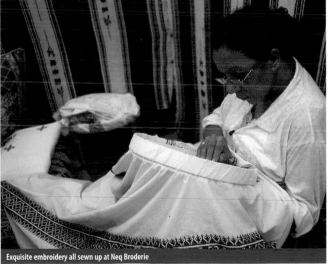
**Exquisite embroidery all sewn up at Neq Broderie**

## WHAT ARE THEY DOING?

A man ties a thread to a nail 1.5m up a wall and runs the thread tautly along the wall for about 15m. A small motor whirrs in his hands. Curious. In fact he's spinning thread for the embroiderers of caftans and jellabas, and for the tiny buttons that adorn these garments. There's a great tradition of making passementerie in Fez: tassels for cushions, buttons for clothing and to decorate *babouches* (leather slippers), heavily embroidered belts for caftans, and to add to prayer beads. Be careful not to walk too close to the wall!

Talaa Kebira. And he can arrange for you to have henna applied by a local henna artist (see p73).

### PARFUMERIE MOULAY IDRISS *Perfumes & Incense*
☎ 035 633995; 39 Souk Triba, Talaa Kebira, Attarine; ⏰ 9am-8pm Sat-Thu
Stocking the usual range of essential oils and mock perfumes, this shop is more interesting for its wide range of prayer beads: the olive wood–and-bone rosary is particularly beautiful (Dh120). There's also gum arabic incense and chunks of sandalwood (per gram Dh30).

### SALON DE THÉ BATHA *Food & Drink*
9 Allal Fassi Avenue, Batha; ⏰ 7.30am-5pm
Here's one of the best patisseries selling excellent bread, cakes and croissants but the *pièce de résistance* is the patisserie: tiny exquisite biscuit creations featuring almonds, sesame paste, chocolate and macaroons. A 250g box of

the best (essential when visiting Moroccan families) costs Dh30 and a mixed platter Dh90.

### SEMLALI MOHAMED *Musical Instruments*
☎ 065 032719; 142 Talaa Kebira; ⏰ 8am-8pm Sat-Thu
In his tiny shop crammed full of musical instruments, Si Mohamed will show you professional quality *ouds* starting at Dh2000, a hennaed goatskin *daf* (handheld drum) at Dh50 or a ceramic *tam-tam* drum from Dh70. There are *gimbris* (a type of lute) from Dh150, depending on size, as well as wooden oboes and Gnaoua castanets.

### SMAIL WAZZANI *Leather*
☎ 063 115435; 28 Zqaq Lehjar, Talaa Seghira; ⏰ 9am-7pm Sat-Thu
This small shop stocks goodquality leather jackets for men (around Dh800) or women (from about Dh750). Jamila Khadiri will also make to order.

## 🔲 SPICE SHOP *Herbs & Spices*

**51 Talaa Kebira;** ⏲ **9am-7pm Sat-Thu**
Hassan Graoui and his son Khalid are justly proud of their emporium of spices. This is an excellent place to stock up on *ras el-hanoot* (shopkeeper's spice mixture) that Hassan grinds himself, from his own secret blend of cinnamon, mace flowers, star anise, turmeric, nutmeg, black pepper, coriander and more (100g Dh50). Perfect for Moroccan cooking.

## 🔲 TISSAGE BERBERE
*Carpets & Leather*

☎ **064 154078; 36 Zqaq Lehjar, Talaa Seghira, Kissariat;** ⏲ **8am or 9am-11pm Sat-Thu**
Koko's shop is chock full of lamps, carpets, blankets and *hendiras*. His speciality is making pouffes to order out of the softest goatskin (non-smelly) with your choice of kilim inserts – old or new. He also has some ready made, and at Dh350 for the large ones, they're a steal.

A fragrant assortment of herbs and spices at the Spice Shop

## 📷 WEDDING CLOTHES SHOP
*Textiles & Embroidery*
☎ 064 093500; 24 Chemmaine Souk;
🕒 9am-8pm Sat-Thu
The souk specialises in wedding outfits. Hassan Bouazzaoui stocks hand-embroidered velvet wedding caftans in every colour (around Dh900), as well as embroidered wedding belts (from Dh100). It's a good place to buy a fez (Dh20).

## 📷 WOODWORK SHOP
*Woodwork*
270 Talaa Kebira; 🕒 10am-7pm Sat-Thu
One of the last craftsmen left who works entirely by hand (and foot), this elderly gentleman produces cedarwood and thuja boxes often inlaid with lemon wood (from Dh60), photograph frames and games such as dominoes (Dh100) and chessboards (from Dh200). He's particularly proud of his

puzzle-boxes – see if you can find out how to open one.

# 🍴 EAT
Moroccan food is justly famous – and one of the best reasons for a visit to Fez is the revered Fassi cuisine. An absolute must is dinner at a riad in the medina. Reasonably priced restaurants are clustered around Bab Bou Jeloud.

## 🍴 CAFÉ CLOCK
*Modern European*                    $$
☎ 061 183264; www.cafeclock.com;
7 Derb el-Margana; 🕒 9am-11pm; Ⓥ
This eclectic café-restaurant, off Talaa Kebira at the Water Clock (p50), offers delicious breakfast, lunch and dinner. Stop for tea and scrumptious cakes (especially the lemon tart) on the roof terrace with its stunning view of the Bou Inania minaret, browse in the book

### MEDINA RESTAURANTS
> Street food is good: hole-in-the-wall stands abound. Sometimes you'll find a stall selling snails in spicy broth, with safety pins to pull out the snail meat (per bowl Dh10), or *harira* (tomato soup with chickpeas) stands where a bowl of steaming soup comes for Dh2.
> There are some so-called 'palace restaurants' dotted around the medina, but they cannot be recommended. The food and service is mediocre and over-priced, and the restaurants are full of large tour groups, often with tacky 'entertainment'.
> Fortunately though, there are some top-notch restaurants perfect for trying Moroccan cuisine, such as La Maison Bleue (opposite). Some of the traditional riads have excellent restaurants, particularly Riad Fes (p67), Dar Anebar (opposite), Ryad Mabrouka (p68), Riyad Sheherazade (p68) and Dar el-Ghalia (opposite). You can dine at these riads even if you're not staying there, as long as you book ahead.

exchange and check out the art on the walls. Try crunchy salads, camel burgers or fresh fish of the day.

### 🍴 DAR ANEBAR
*Moroccan* $$$
☎ 035 635785; www.daranebar.com; 25 Derb el-Miter, Zenjfour, Bab Guissa; 🕑 dinner from 7.30pm

After a drink in the pretty lamp-lit courtyard, retire to one of the sumptuous dining salons to eat Moroccan-style at low tables. Excellent food and friendly service make for an enjoyable evening. Dinner is a set three-course menu, and there's wine.

### 🍴 DAR EL-GHALIA
*Moroccan* $$$
☎ 035 741574; www.riadelghalia.com; 13/15 Ras Rhe, R'cif; 🕑 lunch & dinner

Eat on the terrace or in the salon at this lovely guesthouse. Choose from the set menus or *à la carte*: there are salads, excellent *harira*, grills, fresh fish, tajines and couscous. Order in advance if you'd like to try pigeon *trid* (baked dough stuffed with meat) or *m'choui* (roast lamb). Wines and spirits available. A 10% tip is added to the bill.

### 🍴 DAR ROUMANA
*Modern European* $$$
☎ 035 741637; www.darroumana .com; 30 Derb el-Amer, Zqaq Rommane; 🕑 dinner 7.30pm-9.30pm Tue-Sat; **V**

This is fusion cuisine – Mediterranean food with a Moroccan twist. Dine on the terrace with fabulous views over the medina, or by the fire in winter. Shrimp and sea bass *b'stilla* (rich savoury-sweet pie) or swordfish in pomegranate molasses could tickle your tastebuds, followed by chocolate-and-cinnamon mousse. Book in advance. Wine is available.

### 🍴 KASBAH RESTAURANT
*Moroccan* $
☎ 035 741533; 18 Serrajine, Bou Jeloud; 🕑 8am-midnight

This restaurant is noteworthy for the view and the good selection of local music. The food is somewhat bland, but it's a good place to relax over a glass of mint tea (Dh5). Note that the price of drinks doubles if you're not eating. Choose from the three-course set menu or *à la carte*. Closing hours can extend to when everyone's left!

### 🍴 LA MAISON BLEUE
*Moroccan* $$$
☎ 035 636052; Pl de l'Independence, Batha; 🕑 dinner from 7.30pm; **V**

Billed as 'one of the most romantic hotels in the world', this restaurant lives up to that ideal, with your name spelled out in spangles on the table. An array of salads is followed by a tajine, couscous or *b'stilla* (rich, savoury-sweet

NEIGHBOURHOODS

THE MEDINA

Get all the ingredients for your own Moroccan feast at a produce market

chicken or pigeon pie made with fine pastry), and the signature dessert is *waraka* (a paper-thin pastry, finer than filo, that's crispy when cooked) filled with patisserie cream. As you dine, the *oud*-player strums, interspersed with (gentle) Gnaoua music. Dinner, a set menu, is Dh550 including wine, and it's a good idea to book ahead. Vegetarian meals are available on request.

### 🍴 PALAIS JAMAÏ
*French & Moroccan* $$$
☎ 035 634331; Bab Guissa; 🕙 lunch & dinner; Ⓥ
This five-star hotel has a superb position overlooking the medina. There's a French restaurant and

### FRESH PRODUCE MARKETS

Even if you're not shopping, it's worth wandering the bustling fresh-produce markets in the morning. The best is R'cif market, as well as Bou Jeloud at the top of Talaa Kebira and the lesser known Jouteya in Sagha. The *kissariat* (covered markets) sell seasonal organic fruits and vegetables just like they used to look and taste – this juicy produce doesn't conform to the strict requirements of shape, size and form found in Western supermarkets. There are stalls selling olives, dried fruit and nuts, spices and coffee beans, homemade yogurt and soft cheese and lots of different types of bread, others have gleaming fish for sale (particularly in R'cif) and some vendors squat on the pavement with loose eggs and fresh herbs. For the non-squeamish, there are camel and sheep heads, cows' trotters, bulls' testicles and various innards. The live chickens, turkeys and pigeons will soon have their necks wrung, and those cute bunny rabbits will end up in a tajine.

a Moroccan restaurant. At lunch they serve a good buffet on the terrace above the pool (or in the dining room in winter): there's the salad buffet, or the salad buffet with barbecue and dessert.

### RESTAURANT BOUAYAD
*Moroccan* $

☎ 065 624687; 26 Serrajine, Bou Jeloud; ⏱ 10am-11pm; **V**

Despite its rather soulless interior, this is a good place for a rest (with air-conditioning and clean toilets). It serves a very good fish tajine. Choose from the three-course set menu or *à la carte*.

### RESTAURANT DES JEUNES
*Moroccan* $

☎ 066 880874; 18 Serrajine, Bou Jeloud; ⏱ 5am-1am

A simple pavement café, just inside the bab, with a ready supply of mint tea (Dh5). Restaurant des

Jeunes serves good spit-roast chicken, tajines and couscous. There's a set menu of soup or salad, main dish and dessert.

### RESTAURANT FASSI
*Food Stand* $

33 Sejjarine, Bou Jeloud; ⏱ 10am-10pm

Abdou and his brothers serve excellent sandwiches cooked to order. Choose from the display of meat or chicken with onions and tomatoes and an array of salads, all stuffed into a round loaf or a baguette.

### RIAD FES
*Moroccan* $$$

☎ 035 947610; www.riadfes.com; Derb ben Slimane, Zerbtana; ⏱ dinner; **V**

Dine outside in the courtyard around the pool, or in the elegant restaurant in the new part of the house. There is a three- or four-course set menu. An *oud*-player plays in the dining room. After dinner you can retire to the smoking room or to L'Alcazar (p71).

### 🍴 RIAD SHEHERAZADE

*Moroccan* $$$

☎ 035 741642; www.sheheraz.com; 23 Arsat Bennis, Douh; 🕙 dinner; Ⓥ

A pretty conservatory by the pool serves as a dining room, or you can dine in the large courtyard or Moroccan salon. A speciality of the house is couscous with quails and chicken, studded with fruit. Wine is available. If the owner's in town, he might serenade you with his *oud*.

### 🍴 RYAD MABROUKA

*Moroccan* $$$

☎ 035 636345; Derb el-Miter, Ain Azleten; 🕙 dinner from 8pm-9.30pm; Ⓥ

Dine in the leafy garden of this delightful riad guesthouse in the warmer months, or in winter in the 1st-floor dining room overlooking the medina. Traditional fare is served in a three-course set menu, and wine is available. It's necessary to book 24 hours in advance.

### 🍴 SANDWICHES BIG MAC

*Food Stand* $

3 Talaa Seghira; 🕙 10am-10pm

It's certainly fast food, but there are no Big Macs here! Choose from the display cabinet and watch your sandwich filling being cooked on the griddle. Stuffed baguettes or bread rounds come with chips. There are some chairs and tables, too, for tea or coffee (both Dh4).

### 🍴 SNAIL STAND

*Food Stand* $

cnr Talaa Seghira & Derb el-Horra; 🕙 5pm-10pm

Bahou Hasnaoui serves a good bowl of snails. Ease out the little critters from their shells with the safety pin provided. The broth is spicy and aromatic and is said to keep colds away. Note that opening hours can vary.

### 🍴 THAMI'S *Moroccan* $

☎ 070 640130; 50 Serrajine, Bou Jeloud; 🕙 8.30am or 9am-11pm; Ⓥ

This pavement restaurant has just two tables: one for 12 people to share, and one for just two or three. Thami produces an excellent *kefta* tajine with egg, vegetable plate of *fuul* (broad beans), lentils, aubergines and peppers, couscous and *makoda* (potato fritters) with *harissa* (hot sauce made with red chillies and red peppers) dip. Drinks include tea, coffee or freshly squeezed orange juice.

# 🍸 DRINK

There might be 350 mosques in the medina, but it's impossible to count the number of cafés – there seems to be one on every corner.

They're great places to soak up the atmosphere and do some people-watching. When nothing but a beer will quench your thirst, head for the hotels on the outskirts (alcohol is not available in the medina, except in a few restaurants).

## �Y CAFÉ BA BOUCHTA *Café*
**Sagha Sq, Sagha; ** 🕑 7am-9pm
Opposite the *funduq* is this very old café. A small wood fire, pumped up with bellows, heats water in a copper urn; sugar is chipped off a large cone with a special hammer, and men sit playing cards in the L-shaped room. Sit on a stool at the window and watch the square below. Mint tea is Dh2.50 and coffee Dh3.

## �Y CAFE DE TABARAKALLAH *Café*
**Blvd Ahmed ben Mohamed Alaoui, R'cif;** 🕑 5.30am-10pm
This large popular café, opposite Cinema Amal, has space inside and upstairs, but the best place for watching the world go by is outside on the pavement. *Pains au chocolat* (pastry with chocolate) are Dh2, coffee or mint tea Dh5.

## �Y CAFE FIRDAOUS *Café*
**Pl de l'Independence, Batha;** 🕑 5.45am-9.30pm
This is a great place for breakfast (croissant Dh3, *pain au chocolat*

Dh2, coffee Dh5), or sip a glass of mint tea (Dh5) and watch the comings and goings in bustling Batha.

## �Y CAFE KORTOBA *Café*
**Derb Boutouil;** 🕑 9am-6pm Sat-Thu
This café is an institution. When you get tired of all the walking, it is a great (albeit small) place to sit a while for coffee or mint tea (Dh4), orange juice (Dh5), an ice cream (Dh6) or a slice of cake (Dh10.50). Bang on the edge of the Kairaouine, you'll find there's plenty going on around you.

## �Y CREMERIE LA PLACE *Café*
**Seffarine Sq;** 🕑 7.30am-8.30pm Sat-Thu
This is one of the best people-watching spots in the medina. Friendly Mostapha serves excellent mint tea or coffee (both Dh6), freshly squeezed orange juice (large Dh8) and pastries. Sit on stools in the tiny space inside, or spread out on the pavement in this prettiest of squares and watch the coppersmiths hammering away, and the passing parade.

## �Y HOTEL BATHA *Bar*
☎ 035 634860; Pl de l'Independence, Batha
The only hotel inside the medina, the Batha is a welcome relief if you'd like a beer, bottle of wine or gin and tonic. In winter, the

Now that's a view – Hotel Les Merinides

cosy Churchill Bar (10am to 10pm) has two roaring fires to snuggle around. There's one courtyard by the pool for daytime and early evenings. The courtyard and the Consul Bar (11am to midnight; see opposite) at the back of the hotel is a good place for a drink later in the evening. During happy 'hour' (5pm to 9pm) two beers come for the price of one.

### ☐ HOTEL LES MERINIDES *Bar*
☎ 035 646040; Borj Nord; ☾ bar 8am-11pm

This large hotel overlooking the medina sports the best terrace view; it's good for a pre-prandial drink. The terrace has comfortable seating and is served by waiters from the bar. There's live music in the evening. Local beer is Dh20; a gin and tonic Dh40.

## ⛉ L'ALCAZAR *Bar*

☎ 035 741012; www.riadfes.com;
**Riad Fes, 5 Derb ben Slimane, Zerbtana,
Batha;** ⏱ 8am-10.30pm

The owner-architect designed the
new courtyard with plasterwork
copied from the Alhambra. This
bar, at Riad Fes (p67), faces a
decorative pool and it's all very
modern, with a Moroccan twist.
Wine is available by the glass in
this relaxing environment, as well
as other tipples.

## ⛉ NEJJARINE MUSEUM CAFÉ
*Café*

**Nejjarine Sq;** ⏱ 10am-7pm

On the roof terrace of the museum, this café serves drinks only
(everything Dh10) and is a great
place for gazing out over the
rooftops of the nearby Kairaouine
and Moulay Idriss Zawiya. Sit
outside, or in an air-conditioned
room. Not cheap with the museum entrance fee as well, but it's
worth it for the friendly service
and clean toilets.

## ⛉ PALAIS JAMAÏ HOTEL *Bar*

☎ 035 634331; www.sofitel.com; **Bab
Guissa;** ⏱ 10am-midnight

Enjoy a drink on the terrace or
in the piano lounge of the Palais
Jamaï (p66). The service is slow.
Note that the high prices charged
for drinks before dinner include a
wide selection of snacks.

# ★ PLAY

## ⭐ AIN AZLETEN HAMMAM
*Hammams & Spas*

**Talaa Kebira, Ain Azleten;** ⏱ men
**6am-noon & 8.30pm-11pm, women
noon-8.30pm**

Probably the cleanest public hammam, this bathhouse has recently
been renovated. It costs around
Dh40, including soap and *ghassoul,* for a session here; and the
attendants will scrub, rinse and
massage you.

## ⭐ CONSUL BAR *Bar*

☎ 035 741077; **Hotel Batha, Pl de
l'Independence, Batha;** ⏱ disco 9pm-
**midnight Tue-Sun**

So named because it was once
the British Consulate (before it
became a bar, that is), the Consul
at the back of the Hotel Batha
(p69) has music and a widescreen
TV after 9pm – and thus calls
itself a disco.

## ⭐ FÈS PALAIS D'HÔTES SPA
ANDALOUS *Hammams & Spas*

☎ 035 637324/33; www.palais-hotes
**.com; Derb Sornas, Ziat;** ⏱ 8.30am-9pm

This sumptuous spa attached to
a guesthouse sports an indoor
pool, gym and hammam and
offers various beauty treatments.
A hammam with *gommage* costs
Dh500, or spend the whole day
with aquacise in the pool (towels

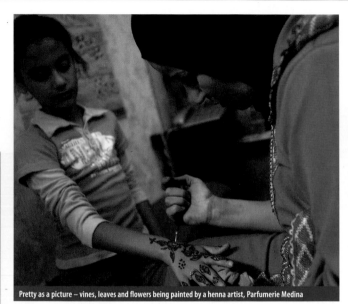

Pretty as a picture – vines, leaves and flowers being painted by a henna artist, Parfumerie Medina

provided), sauna, Jacuzzi, gym and a massage for Dh1000. After all that you'll need the free tisane, mineral water or juice on offer.

### ⭐ LES MUSICALES DU PALAIS EL-MOKRI *Concerts*

☎ 068 601791; www.lesmusicalesdefes .com in French; Mokri Palace, Chaq Bden- jala, Ziat; admission Dh60; ☽ 4-6pm Wed & Sun

Traditional music concerts held at the Mokri Palace (p48) salons are a delight: feast your eyes on the spectacular surroundings and im- agine yourself a pasha of old. See the website for the programme of events and groups performing (except in August). The entrance fee includes tea and Moroccan pastries.

### ⭐ MASSAGE MAROC
*Hammams & Spas*

☎ 068 823040; www.massagemaroc .com in French; 9 Derb Moulay Ismail

Frenchwoman Celine Vlaminck is trained in Ayurvedic massage, reiki and reflexology, and a 1½-hour treatment costs Dh350. Check the website for details of courses, which take place at Celine's medina house, off Talaa Seghira: massage, Kundalini yoga, meditation, movement and nonviolent communication.

### ⭐ PARFUMERIE MEDINA
*Hammams & Spas*
☎ 035 636009; 7 Henna Souk, Derb Fakharine; ⏲ 9am-7pm
If you've always hankered after arabesques swirling round fingers and wrists and even toes and ankles, here's the ideal place. The henna artist applies the mixture while you relax under the plane tree in the Henna Souk, off Talaa Kebira. She charges Dh30 for a finger-and-wrist design, or Dh200 for the full treatment of hands, forearms and feet.

### ⭐ RIAD ALKANTARA
*Hammams & Spas, Concerts*
☎ 035 740292; www.riadalkantara .com; 24 Oued Souaffine, Douh
A complex of six grand houses around a pool and garden, Riad Alkantara was due to open early in 2008. There are workshops in Moroccan crafts, art workshops for children, a café and evenings

of poetry, storytelling and music. The spa (opening late 2008) has a hammam and massage room, and offers classes in movement, yoga and meditation.

### ⭐ RIAD MAISON BLEUE SPA
*Hammams & Spas*
☎ 035 741873; resa@maisonbleue .com; 31 Derb el-Miter, Ain Azleten; ⏲ 10.30am-8.30pm
This spa uses Moroccan products such as *ghassoul*, argan oil, orange flower water and rose petals. The basic hammam treatment costs DH500, a session including the steam room, *gommage* (exfoliation) and massage costs Dh800; the Thousand & One Nights treatment adds a manicure, pedicure and facial (Dh1900).

### ⭐ SEFFARINE HAMMAM
*Hammams & Spas*
Seffarine Sq; ⏲ men 6am midnight, women 8am-10pm
There are separate hammams here for men and women, both with beautifully domed ceilings. It costs around Dh40, including a tip. The Venice Institute for Urban Sustainability has chosen one hammam to restore in cities such as Tunis, Damascus and Gaza – and this one in Fez.

# >FEZ EL-JDID

When you consider that this neighbourhood was established by the Merinids over 700 years ago, its name (New Fez) is somewhat misleading! Enclosed by massive fortified ramparts, it has four main areas. To the west is the sprawling Royal Palace, which is out-of-bounds to tourists. Its handsome gilt-bronze main gate fronts Alaouites Sq – if you're coming from the Ville Nouvelle or from the medina, consider catching a petit taxi to this square and starting your exploration here. To the east of the square is the historically important Mellah (Jewish quarter). At the Mellah's northern point is the monumental Bab Semmarine, gateway to the neighbourhood's main artery, Derb Fez el-Jdid. The crowded laneways to either side of this street are home to mosques, artisans' workshops and houses. At the northern end of Derb Fez el-Jdid is the impressive Moulay Hassan Sq, and off this square to the southwest is the extremely poor and religiously conservative area of Moulay Abdallah.

## FEZ EL-JDID

### ◉ SEE

### ☐ SHOP

### ⍩ EAT

### ▼ DRINK

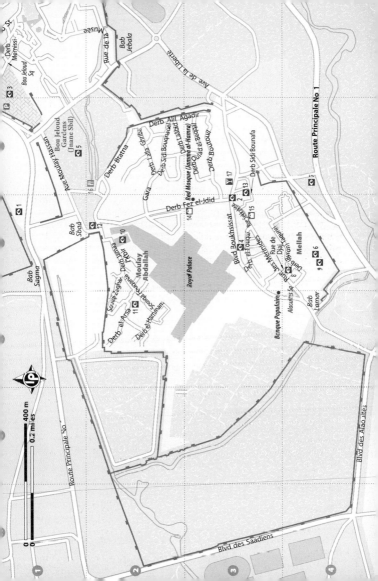

# 👁 SEE

## 👁 ABOU BAKR IBN ARABI MAUSOLEUM

Abou Bakr ibn Arabi arrived in Fez from Seville in the 11th century. An *ala* (learned man) and an imam, he was on a pilgrimage to meet all of the renowned *ulama* (Islamic scholars) of his day. So taken was he with the learned atmosphere of Fez that he returned here after his trip. When he died, the Fassis built this mausoleum with its green-tiled dome to honour his memory. You'll find it just outside the medina ramparts, to the east of Bab Sagma.

## 👁 BAB SEMMARINE

This 13th-century gateway was originally called Uyune Sanhaja (the Springs of Sanhaja) in honour of an important Moroccan Berber tribe. Built to house the storage silos of the Merenid city, it was modified in the 20th century to facilitate traffic and people movement. On its eastern side is one of the city's main produce souks.

## 👁 BAGHDADI SQUARE

The local tourism authorities like to spruik this square as being the local equivalent of Marrakesh's Djemaa el-Fna. This is wishful thinking on their part, but the square is worthy of an early evening wander during festival periods, when it's colonised by street entertainers and hawkers selling traditional remedies.

## 👁 BOU JELOUD GARDENS
**Ave Moulay Hassan**

Fassis were overjoyed when Moulay Hassan opened these 18th-century gardens (also known as Jnane Sbil) to the public in the 19th century. They have flocked here ever since to admire the ornamental plantings, relax under perfumed orange trees and wan-

---

### THE BEATIFIED EXPLORER

Derb el-Fouqui, off Rue des Mérinides, was where wealthy Jews chose to build opulent mansions in the heyday of the Mellah (Jewish quarter). Charles de Foucauld (1858–1916), the Catholic religious leader who inspired the founding of the Little Brothers of Jesus, stayed in one of these mansions when he visited Fez in 1883. De Foucault, who spoke Arabic, Hebrew and Tuareg, was fascinated with North Africa and decided to explore the region after resigning from his commission with an Algerian-based regiment of the French army. He travelled through Morocco in 1883 and 1884 disguised as a rabbi; his reconnaissance of the country later earned him the Gold Medal of the French Geographical Society.

French-period architecture on Rue des Mérinides

der along the banks of tributaries of the Oued Fès. The gardens were being renovated at the time of research.

### ◉ BOULEVARD BOUKHSISSAT

The picturesque buildings that line this street date from the period of the French Mandate. Cream-coloured and with brown-painted balconies, they were designed to provide housing on the 1st floor and shops on the ground floor, an arrangement that continues to this day.

### ◉ DERB FEZ EL-JDID

Once the centre of the city's socio-economic activities, this bustling thoroughfare dates to the start of the 14th century and was home to souks, *funduqs* (caravanseries), hammams, *farranes* (communal ovens), fountains and the *rahba zraâ* (wheat market). These days it's home to *kissariat* (covered markets) selling everything from jellabas to jewellery. The 14th-century mosque with the attractive green-tiled minaret is known as the **Jamaa al-Hamra** (Red Mosque). Go figure.

### ◉ FONDOUK AMERICAIN
☎ 035 931953; www.fondouk.org;
🕑 7.30am-1pm Mon-Fri

This animal hospital was estab-lished in 1927 at the instigation of Amy Bend Bishop, an American traveller who was appalled at the poor condition of the many work-ing animals in the medina. A team headed by Canadian veterinarian Denis Frappier treats the city's animals free of charge, courtesy of funding from The Massachu-setts Society for the Prevention of Cruelty to Animals. In a country where many humans cannot easily access medical care, veterinary care is often viewed as a luxury, so the work of charities such as this one is extremely important, par-ticularly as many locals rely on the their animals to transport goods,

### Dr Armand Guigui
*President of the Jewish community in Fez*

**How many Jews live in the Mellah today?** None at all. The 200 Jews left in Fez all live in the Ville Nouvelle. At the beginning of the 1940s there were 30,000 Jews living here, but many members of our community left at the creation of Israel; others left at Independence (1956). **What parts of the Mellah are of the greatest significance for visitors interested in Fez's Jewish heritage?** The four 17th-century synagogues and the cemetery. The synagogues are the Ibn Danan (opposite), El-Fassiniyine, El-Mansano, and Em Habanim (opposite). **Have all of these synagogues been restored?** The Ibn Danan has been restored and functions as a museum. The other three synagogues will be refurbished in the order I mentioned them in. They are all classified as historic monuments by Unesco and the Ministry of Culture. **Do any of these synagogues still function?** No. There are two synagogues in the Ville Nouvelle that cater to the local community.
*Interview by Helen Ranger*

carry water and help with the harvesting of crops. The hospital welcomes visitors and gratefully accepts donations.

## ◉ IBN DANAN SYNAGOGUE

**Rue de Djaj, off Rue des Mérinides; admission by donation; ⏲ 7am-7pm**

An enthusiastic caretaker will shepherd you through this unassuming but pretty synagogue, which is one of the oldest and most important in North Africa. Built and owned by a prominent Moroccan Jewish family in the mid-17th century, it was renovated to its present form at the end of the 19th century. The synagogue contains what is thought to be the only complete set of Moroccan synagogue fittings in existence, including a *tevah* (reader's canopy platform made from wood and wrought iron), *hechal* (twin carved-wood arks for the Torah), wooden benches, chairs (including Elijah's Chair for the circumcision ceremony) and embroidered hangings. Restored in recent years after being listed on the World Monument Fund's list of the world's 100 most endangered cultural heritage sites, it provides a fascinating glimpse into the rich Jewish history of the Mellah (see p15 for more information). Note that the synagogue is closed on Fridays during Muslim prayer time and for Shabbat.

## ◉ JEWISH CEMETERY & EM HABANIM SYNAGOGUE

**Admission by donation, usually Dh10; ⏲ 7.30am-7.30pm**

Generations of Fassi Jews are buried in this impeccably maintained cemetery, off Bab Lamar. Regimented lines of humble whitewashed tombs bearing the venerable names of Cohen, Danan, Hassarfati and Gabay parade down the hill toward the main road. In the centre, recognisable by its green urns, is the tomb of the 19th-century martyr Solica, a 17-year-old girl who refused to convert to Islam or accept the advances of the Governor of Tangier and had her throat slit as a result. The Em Habanim Synagogue at the far end of the cemetery is now home to a modest museum of Jewish history, but it is rarely open.

## ◉ L'KBIR MOSQUE

**Derb Jamaa l'Kbir**

Fez el-Djid's 'Grand Mosque' was built in the 13th century by the Merenid sultan Moulay Abou Youseef Yacoub and was subsequently used as a mausoleum for the sultans Abou Said and Abou Inan. Its architect was clearly influenced by the Kairaouine – peek into the courtyard to admire the lovely green tiles and delicate decorative plasterwork.

## MOULAY ABDALLAH MAUSOLEUM
**Derb el-Arsa**

This 17th-century mosque and *medersa* (theological college) was converted into a mausoleum in the 18th century and is the resting place of four sultans of the reigning Alawite dynasty: Moulay Abdallah, Moulay Youssef, Moulay Hafid and Moulay Abdelaziz. Non-Muslims cannot enter.

## MOULAY HASSAN SQUARE

Created towards the end of the 19th century by order of the Alawite sultan Moulay al-Hassan I, this impressive square is surrounded by high pisé walls. The northern gate of the royal palace, known as Bab Makhzen, is here, as is the monumental Bab Sbaâ (the Lion Gate, aka Bab Dkaken), which features three solid arches flanked by two towers. Walk through Bab Sbaâ to see Bab al-Makina, the *mechouar* (assembly place) that is the main venue for the Fes Festival of World Sacred Music (p12). Fronting the *mechouar* is Dar Makina, a muscular European-influenced building dating from 1886. Designed by Italian architects and engineers, it was built to house the imperial arsenal. Behind the *mechouar* is Bab Sagma, a gateway bearing the name of a pious woman who was buried on this site in 1737. Its

exterior façade is decorated with long cursive inscriptions on *zellij* (mosaic tilework).

## SIDI BOUNAFA MAUSOLEUM
**Derb Sidi Bounafa**

This mausoleum is said to be a favourite of the city's prostitutes, who make pilgrimages here to ask the saint for help when leaving the world's oldest profession.

# 🛍 SHOP

## DERB FEZ EL-JDID *Clothing*

The *kissariat* along this bustling thoroughfare are home to stalls selling jellabas of every possible colour, quality, price and cut. Utilitarian polyester and wool styles predominate, but it's also possible to access Bollywood-style confections in satin and silk, as well as truly frightening faux–leopard-skin numbers.

## RUE SEKKAKINE *Jewellery*

For centuries, trading in gold or silver was forbidden to Muslims. This was because working precious metals to be sold at higher prices than their base value was considered usury, something forbidden under Islamic law. Jews faced no such prohibitions, though; when members of Fez's Jewish community moved into the Mellah in the 14th century

Relaxing in the tranquil courtyard of the Café Restaurant La Noria

they set up goldsmithing businesses in Rue Sekkakine. Originally patronised by the palace, these days the shops are run by Muslims and cater to the locals' penchant for bling, specialising in jewellery made from garish yellow gold and sparkly stones of every description.

# EAT
## CAFÉ RESTAURANT
**LA NORIA** *Moroccan* $$
☎ 072 421699; 43 Derb Btatna;
⏲ 7am-9.30pm; V

This tranquil courtyard restaurant is tucked away behind the Bou Jeloud gardens, next to a derelict waterwheel. You can sit under orange trees next to the fountain and simply relax over a mint tea (Dh7), or opt for one of the well-priced lunch and dinner set menus. The *tajine poulet au citron*

(tajine of chicken with lemon) is particularly delicious.

# DRINK
## CAFÉ OURIKA *Café*
**Blvd Boukhsissat**
The kerbside tables at this café east of Bab Semmarine are the perfect spots from which to observe the comings and goings of the Mellah. A large mint tea costs Dh10.

## MEDINA CAFÉ *Café*
☎ 035 633430; 6 Derb Mernissi;
⏲ 8.30am-11pm
Nestling in the shadow of Bab Bou Jeloud, this pretty café is a good choice if you feel in need of a restorative mint tea (Dh12) or coffee (Dh10) after battling the medina crowds. Its clean toilets and friendly service deserve commendation, but the food on offer can be disappointing.

# >AL-ANDALOUS

Named after the immigrant community that arrived in Fez from Islamic Spain in the 9th century and settled on this eastern side of the Oued Fès, Al-Andalous is well and truly off the tourist trail. It is centred on the magnificent Al-Andalous Mosque (Jamaâ Andalous), and boasts two of the most architecturally and culturally significant *medersas* (theological colleges) in the city: the Sahrij and the Sbaiyine, both of which date from the 14th century. To explore this quarter, catch a taxi to Bab Fettouh and make your way down Aqbat Sidi Ali Boughaleb; or start at Bab R'cif and climb up Derbs Nekhaline, Jama'a Chouk and Seffah to the mosque. On your peregrination, you'll observe Fassi housewives haggling with local shopkeepers, giggling groups of urchins playing games on the streets and workers enjoying a natter and a hard-earned glass of tea in front of hole-in-the-wall cafés. Touts and tourist tat are nowhere to be seen.

## AL- ANDALOUS

### ⊙ SEE
Al-Andalous
  Mosque ......................**1** B4
Al-Oued Mosque ............**2** B5
Bab Fettouh ..................**3** D6

Sahrij Medersa ...............**4** B5
Sbaiyine Medersa...........**5** B4

### 🛍 SHOP
Dar Tazi............................**6** A5

### 🍴 EAT
Palais de Fes Dar Tazi .....**7** A6

# ◉ SEE

## ◉ AL-ANDALOUS MOSQUE

**Jamaâ Andalous; Souk Jamaa Andalous**
One of the two great mosques of
Fez, this started life as a relatively modest structure in the 9th
century (see right), but became
the congregational mosque of
the quarter in the 10th century.
Its minaret, a gift from the caliph
of Córdoba, dates from 956 and
is very similar to that of its sister
mosque, the Kairaouine. The
mosque was totally rebuilt by the
Almohads between 1203 and 1207
and the magnificent monumental
door on the northern façade dates
from this time. Designed and built
by artisans from the Nasrid king-
dom of Granada, the triple-entry
wooden door features colourful
*zellij* (mosaic tilework), ornate
decorative plasterwork and a huge
cornice of carved cedarwood.
Though everyone can marvel at
the door, only Muslims may enter
the mosque.

## ◉ AL-OUED MOSQUE

**Jamaâ Lranja; Derb L'Mdersa**
The rectangular courtyard of this
18th-century mosque is home
to an assortment of fruit trees,
and once had a stretch of the
Masmouda River flowing through
it (this was covered last century).
The mosque itself, which is also
known as the Lranja Mosque, was

---

### SISTERS DOING IT FOR THEMSELVES

The two great mosques of Fez – the
Kairaouine and the Al-Andalous – date
from the 9th century and were endowed
by pious sisters Fatima and Meryam Al-
Fihria. The daughters of refugees from
the city of Kairouan in Tunisia, they must
have had fond memories of their birth-
place: Fatima chose to name the mosque
she endowed after it; Meryam named
her mosque after the quarter in which it
was located, which had been settled by
exiles from Córdoba in Andalusia.

---

constructed over the ruins of the
Merinid-era Al-Oued Medersa
(River Medersa).

## ◉ BAB FETTOUH

After the death of Prince Ibn Ateya
Senhai in the 11th century, his
two sons divided responsibility
for ruling the city. Fettouh, the
eldest, who ruled the Al-Andalous
quarter, erected this handsome
gate and named it after himself. It
was rebuilt by the Alawites in the
18th century. Opposite the gate is
the Bab Fettouh Cemetery.

## ◉ SAHRIJ MEDERSA

**Derb Yasmina; admission Dh10;**
**⏱ 9.30am-12.30pm & 2.30-6pm Sat-**
**Thu, 9.30-11.30am & 2.30-6pm Fri**
Taking its present name from
the large rectangular pool or
*sahrij* (basin) in its courtyard,

this *medersa* dates from the 14th century. Built by the Merinid sultan Abou al-Hassan Ali as a theological school attached to the Al-Andalous mosque, it features rich decoration including ornate and exquisite panels of *mashrabiya* (intricate carved wood), *zellij* and decorative plasterwork. The building was designed to lead students from the entrance through the ornate screen door, past the *sahrij* and to the *mihrab* (niche indicating direction of Mecca) in the prayer room opposite the entrance. The Getty Foundation recently funded a conservation analysis of the building, which is in poor structural state, and it is hoped that Getty or another corporation will now step in to fund a full restoration. The medersa was once linked to the neighbouring Sahrij Medersa by an underground passage. See also p13.

## SBAIYINE MEDERSA
### Derb Yasmina
Once called the Medersa al-Soghra (Small Medersa) to distinguish it from the neighbouring Sahrij Medersa (Big Medersa), this building dates from the 14th century and is notable for the decorated marble fountain that graces its interior courtyard. Unfortunately, the building is in a deplorable state of repair and is not open to the public. See also p13.

Calmly reflecting at the Sahrij Medersa

## Badria Fakhkhari
*Art Naji Ceramics Factory*

**What is your role at Art Naji?** I'm responsible for the orders and shipping. **Is it unusual for a Moroccan woman to work in a senior role in a business or company?** In the past, yes. But now women are represented in government and in all businesses and professions. **Is Art Naji a family business?** Yes. My family has run it since 1930, which is three generations. My brothers Naji and Omar and I are the members of the current generation. **Does Art Naji train its own artisans?** Yes, we are a training center as well as a factory. We also run workshops for visitors. **How old are your artisans when they start their training?** They start aged 16 years. **Where do you source your olive pits from?** From olive-oil factories. **Is there a healthy future for the Moroccan ceramic industry?** Business is going well, thank God, and is improving every day.
*Interview by Virginia Maxwell*

## WORTH THE TRIP

After admiring the zillions of zellij tiles that adorn buildings and fountains throughout the medina, you may well decide that some should accompany you home. If this is the case, **Art Naji** ( ☎ 035 669166; www.artnaji.net; 20 Ql, Ain Nokbi; ☯ 8am-6pm) should be your first port of call. This family-run ceramics factory is a 10-minute taxi ride (Dh5) from Bab Fettouh and produces good-quality tabletops, mirrors and fountains encrusted with hand-painted mosaic tiles, as well as pottery plates, bowls and tajines decorated with natural dyes. You can tour the factory and watch the artisans at work – English-speaking staff members are happy to explain the process. The factory can also organise for your purchases to be shipped home.

# 🛍 SHOP

### 🛍 DAR TAZI *Carpets*
☎ 072 761590; 15 Makhfiya Garden, R'cif; ☯ 7am-9.30pm
This large building houses a guesthouse, a restaurant and a ground-floor carpet shop. Drinking mint tea is *de rigueur* while you peruse the rugs of every colour and quality that will be theatrically unfurled at your feet.

# 🍴 EAT

Decent eating and drinking options are scarce in the Al-Andalous quarter. It's best to explore in the morning and make your way back to the medina for lunch.

### 🍴 PALAIS DE FES DAR TAZI
*Moroccan*                          $$$
☎ 072 761590; 15 Makhfiya Garden, R'cif; ☯ lunch & dinner; Ⓥ
Beloved by tour groups, this long-running restaurant offers wonderful views and pricey set menus. Be warned: if you manage to eat your way through the generous array of salads, move onto a main course of tajine (meat and vegetable stew), *brochettes* (kebabs) or *b'stilla aux fruit des mers* (rich, savoury-sweet seafood pie made with fine pastry) and finish with fruit, pastries and tea, you may well have trouble getting up from the table. A service charge of 10% will be added to your bill.

# >VILLE NOUVELLE

The wide boulevards and manicured gardens of Fez's Ville Nouvelle (New Town) are worlds away from the narrow medieval streets of the medina. Constructed by the French as an administrative and residential base, it was conceived as a showcase of the benefits of the Protectorate, and was adorned with grand colonial buildings such as the Bank al-Maghrib on Pl Yacoub al-Mansour (formerly Pl Florence). After independence the prosperous residents of the medina moved here in droves, a trend emulated to this day. The Ville Nouvelle's major boulevards are Ave Hassan II and Blvd Mohammed V. To the northwest of Ave Hassan II is the Gare Ferroviaire (train station); the Gare TCM (bus station) is to the southeast, near Pl Bir Anzarane.

## VILLE NOUVELLE

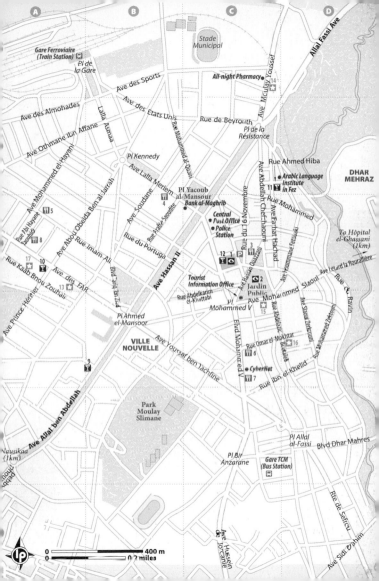

# SEE

## CENTRAL MARKET

**Blvd Mohammed V;** ⏱ **8am-1pm & 2-8.30pm**

Popularly known as the Marché Centrale, this is where serious cooks come to buy their provisions. You won't find any piped music, trolleys or checkout girls with attitude here; instead you'll observe friendly stall owners arranging teetering pyramids of freshly picked vegetables, laying out glistening rows of fish and wielding bloody cleavers in the somewhat confronting meat section. There are plans to move the market to a new location on Rue Arabie Saoudite by 2010, with its current location to host an office block and underground car park.

Pick a spot and enjoy the evening promenade along Ave Hassan II

## A POPULAR PROMENADE

It's approaching the understatement of the century to say that there's not a lot to do in the Ville Nouvelle. No doubt this is why the evening promenade up and down Ave Hassan II has become such a popular form of local entertainment. Over recent years the local government has spent a considerable amount of time and money 'beautifying' the boulevard, and its palm trees, manicured lawns, flower beds and fountains are much admired by the crowds of families, couples and giggling adolescents who strut their stuff along its length, chatting with friends and enjoying seeing and being seen. It's particularly crowded – and loads of fun – when there's a special event or when the king is in town.

### ◎ JARDIN PUBLIC
**cnr Aves Mohammed Slaoui & Mohamed Zerktouni**

If the locals aren't to be found promenading down Ave Hassan II or colonising the terraces at Assouan or Blue Babel, they'll probably be in this manicured public garden close to the Central Market. There's a café, small waterfall, shady trees and plenty of seating.

## 🍴 EAT
### 🍴 CHEAP EATERIES
*Moroccan* $

**Aves Hassan Ouazzani & Abdellah Chef-chaouni;** ☽ **breakfast, lunch & dinner;** Ⓥ

The raft of clean and cheap eateries along this strip near the Jardin Public serve fresh salads, *brochettes* (kebabs) and tajines that could hold their own in many of the city's upmarket restaurants. After eating your fill, it's not unknown to receive change from Dh40. The place closest to the garden is our favourite.

### 🍴 CHICKEN MAC *Moroccan* $
**Ave Lalla Meriem;** ☽ **breakfast, lunch & dinner**

This rotisserie joint south of the train station is a perfect pit stop if you're after a cheap and tasty snack. It doesn't have a street sign, but you'll find it near Sandwich Venizia and La Concorde.

### 🍴 DON PANINI *Moroccan* $
**Rue Imam Ali;** ☽ **breakfast, lunch & dinner;** Ⓥ

For a cheap sandwich or fresh salad, you need go no further than this popular fast-food joint. Locals love it to bits and once you've tasted the food, you'll know why.

### 🍴 LE MAJESTIC
*European* $$$
☎ **035 729999; Route de Zwagha;** ☽ **noon-10pm;** Ⓥ

As swish as the Ville Nouvelle's dining scene gets, this upmarket place in the Henri Leconte Tennis Academy dishes up food that it describes as being 'refined, inventive and modern'. And fair enough, too. It is known for its fish dishes and its truly excellent seasonal salads. The wine list is prohibitively expensive, so it's fortunate that the house wine here is perfectly quaffable. If you call ahead, the restaurant will send a car to collect you from your hotel and drop you back at no cost.

### ☷ LES TROIS SOURCES
*European*                          $$$
☎ 035 606532; Km 4, Route d'Immouzer; ⏱ lunch & dinner
If pressed, locals in the know will 'fess up and say that this cosy French restaurant in the Country Club is their favourite place to eat in Fez. The food is excellent, the wine list is well balanced and the atmosphere is extremely welcoming. The restaurant will collect you from your medina hotel and return you after dinner at no charge if you call in advance.

### ☷ RESTAURANT MARRAKECH
*Moroccan*                           $$
☎ 035 930876; 11 Rue Omar el-Mokhtar; ⏱ noon-10pm; Ⓥ
It's always wise to follow the French when it comes to choosing a dinner venue, and the fact that this welcoming restaurant is always chock-full with Gallic gas-

tronomes is a clear clue as to its quality. The three-course menus on offer include main courses of *couscous royale, brochettes Morocain* or *b'stilla aux poulet* (rich, savoury-sweet chicken pie made with fine pastry). Drawbacks? No alcohol and no credit cards.

### ☷ RESTAURANT ZAGORA
*Moroccan & European*                $$
☎ 035 624618; 5 Blvd Mohammed V; ⏱ noon-10pm; Ⓥ
The kitsch décor featuring naff Kasbah murals will be forgiven the minute you taste the tasty and well-priced dishes on offer at this long-standing favourite. The *m'hammer d'agneau aux légumes* (roast lamb with vegetables and cumin) is simple but perfectly cooked and the fish dishes are equally satisfying. With a good wine list and ultrafriendly waiters, this place is hard to beat. You will find this restaurant at the rear of the arcade.

### ☷ VESUVIO
*European*                         $-$$
☎ 035 624618; 9 Rue Abi Hayane Taouhidi, off Ave des FAR; ⏱ lunch & dinner; Ⓥ
If you're at the stage of screaming when presented with yet another tajine, this place may well be for you. Stock-standard Italian dishes feature – the thin-crust pizzas and

Primed for people-watching – coffee and cake in a Ville Nouvelle café

stodgy pasta are acceptable, but only just. No alcohol.

### 🍴 ZEN GARDEN RESTAURANT LOUNGE *European* $$–$$$
☎ 035 932929; 26 Ave Omar Ibnou Khattab; 🕒 lunch & dinner; Ⓥ
It's chic, it's popular and its prices don't reach into the stratosphere. Pasta or pizza and a bottle of the local *vin rouge* are your best bet here – complicated dishes can be less satisfying. The location is a five-minute drive from the centre of town and taxis can be hard to

come by, so book a pick-up in advance.

## 🍸 DRINK
### 🍸 ASSOUAN *Café*
☎ 035 625851; 4 Ave Allal ben Abdullah
Tables on the terrace of this popular café offer peerless people-watching opportunities. Park yourself here during the promenade hour, order a coffee (espresso Dh8) and slice of gooey gateaux (Dh10) and prepare to enjoy yourself.

**Si Mohamed Baghdadi**
*Coordinator, Arabic Language Institute in Fez (ALIF)*

**Is there a colloquial form of Arabic here in Fez?** Yes, it's called Darija. We teach both Colloquial Moroccan Arabic (CMA) and Modern Standard Arabic (MSA) here. **If a student is interested in learning the most language in the shortest time what would you suggest?** Enrolling in our six-week Darija course and asking us to organise a homestay, where the student stays with a family in the medina and so has a full immersion in both language and culture. **What is your mother tongue?** I am from the Middle Atlas, so my mother tongue is the Berber dialect of Tamazight. I also speak CMA, MSA, Arabic, French and English. **Are the Moroccan dialects widely spoken?** They were in serious danger of dying, but recent efforts to boost awareness through cultural initiatives seem to be leading to a revival. **What do most Fassis speak and read?** Most speak Darija and those who have studied at secondary school can usually speak and read MSA and French as well. Those who have only had one or two years of schooling can read basic Darija only. This is why it's a big problem that there is no Darija newspaper or TV station in Morocco.
*Interview by Virginia Maxwell*

### ⛾ BLUE BABEL *Café*
☎ 035 931406; 22 Ave des FAR

The vibe here is similar to that of Assouan, but the location isn't as good, and the clientele is a bit younger (ice cream and pizza join coffee and cake on the menu). The prices are the same as at Assouan.

### ⛾ CAFÉ JAWHARAT FES *Café*
☎ 035 650992; 16 Ave Farhat Hachad

Staff and students at the nearby American Language Center couldn't believe their luck when this café recently opened its doors. The Gulf-style décor is over-the-top, but the service is friendly and professional, the terrace is pleasant and the coffee isn't bad (Dh7 to Dh8). Best of all, it offers free wi-fi.

### ⛾ CRÉMERIE SKALI *Café*
☎ 035 650992; Blvd Mohammed V; ☽ 6am–10pm

A favourite haunt of traders and shoppers at the Central Market, this unassuming café serves juices (Dh10), coffees (Dh5) and pastries (Dh4). It's a particularly satisfying mid morning stop.

## ⭐ PLAY

### ⛏ CROWN PALACE HOTEL *Bar*
☎ 035 948000; 85 Ave des FAR; ☽ from 6pm

There's not much on offer when it comes to glam nightlife in Fez, so cashed-up locals usually end up partying in the downstairs piano bar or upstairs cigar and cocktail bar at the Crown Palace. When these bars close around 1am, the crowd sometimes relocates to the basement nightclub – the VIP – that has a DJ between midnight and 3am each night.

### ⛏ LE MAROCAIN *Bar*
38 Ave Mohammed Slaoui; ☽ from 9pm

The rear bar of this decidedly louche nightspot is where the city's working girls tout for trade; their male colleagues are usually found preening in the front bar. The band and resident chanteuse aren't likely to be appearing in a concert hall near you in the near future, but they're fun to listen to before you take to the dance floor. Well-priced drinks (beers Dh15) come with tapas-like snacks.

### ⛏ NAUSIKAA SPA *Spa*
☎ 035 610006; www.nausikaa-spa.com; Ave Bahnini, Route Ain Smen16 Ave Farhat Hachad; ☽ 7am–9pm

How do we love thee, Nausikaa? Let us count the ways… We love your luxury fit-out, your relaxing massages (Dh200 to Dh350), your Payot and Thalgo facials (Dh250 to Dh900) and your wide range of body treatments (Dh70 to Dh790). But most of all we love your indulgent hammam experience, particularly as it only costs Dh100, and you can have your hair blow-dried afterwards for Dh40.

## ⭐ ORIENTALIST ART GALLERY
*Gallery*

☎ 035 944545; www.fes-orientalistart gallery.com; 38 Rue Abdelaziz Boutaleb; ⏲ 9.30am-12.30pm & 3.30-7.30pm Mon-Sat

This small commercial gallery is the best place to view the work of contemporary Fez-based artists. The only other option in town is the art gallery in the Délégation de la Culture on Ave Moulay Youssef, close to the Pl de la Résistance, which hosts occasional exhibitions.

## ⭐ YUBA-CYN SPA *Spa*

☎ 035 943506; www.yuba-cyn-spa .com in French; Résidence les Roses-Astoria, 14/16 Rue Kaab Bnou Zouhair; ⏲ 9am-9pm Tue-Sun

A bit of Bangkok recreated in the centre of Fez, Yuba-cyn has become known for its blissful Thai massages (it was the first spa to offer these in Morocco). They cost between Dh150 and Dh400; aromatherapy massages cost Dh300. It also offers aromatherapy treatments, hairdressing, mani-cures, pedicures and waxing for men and women.

> EXCURSIONS

The medina in Meknès is the backdrop to Ave Moulay Ismaïl

# MEKNÈS

Nothing is quite as intoxicating as the experience of visiting one of Morocco's imperial cities. And one of the alluring facts about staying in Fez is that there's a second imperial city a mere hour away. Meknès is smaller and less spectacular than its near neighbour, but its quiet charm inevitably seduces visitors, making it an excellent day or overnight trip.

Arriving in the ville nouvelle (new town) by train, you should catch a taxi to lively **Place el-Hedim** in the ville ancienne (ancient town). This

Ancient granary at Heri es-Souani

large square was built by Sultan Moulay Ismail, who made Meknès the imperial capital after he assumed the throne in 1672. There's no doubt that Moulay Ismail was a nasty piece of work, but he sure knew how to build an imposing city. Monumental walls, gates and a huge **palace complex** (closed to the public) were built by conscripted Christian labourers, as was his utterly extraordinary **Heri es-Souani**, the massive imperial granaries and stables.

The medina in Meknès is smaller but just as labyrinthine as its Fassi equivalent. The shopping possibilities are neither as varied nor as impressive, but the **marché** (produce souk) located on the western side of Place el-Hedim is one of the best in Morocco – row after row of pyramids of spices and pickles, displays of honey-drenched pastries and piles of farm-fresh fruits and vegetables are on display.

In the medina you'll find the delightful **Musee Riad Jamaï**, with its collection of traditional embroidery, jewellery, textiles and ceramics. Housed in a palace built by the powerful Jamaï family, two of whose members were grand viziers to Moulay al-Hassan I, it's well worth a visit. Also worth a stop is the **Medersa Bou Inania** (Qobbat Souk), a run-down but extremely pretty version of the *medersa* (theological college) of the same name in Fez.

## INFORMATION

**Location** 60km southwest of Fez.

**Getting there** Meknès is an easy 50-minute train trip from Fez (1st/2nd class Dh26/18); alight at Meknès Amir Abdelkader. There are 11 trains from Fez per day (first train 1.50am, last train 6.50pm); and 11 returning to Fez daily (first train 9.29am, the last at 1.33am).

**Tourist information** ( ☎ 035 524426; dtmeknes@menara.md; 127 Pl l'Administration; 🕑 8.30am-4.30 Mon-Fri)

**Museum entry** Heri es-Souani (admission Dh10; 🕑 9am-noon & 3-6.30pm); Medersa Bou Inania (Qobbat Souk; admission Dh10; 🕑 9am-6pm); Musee Riad Jamai ( ☎ 055 530863; Pl el-Hedim; adult/child under 12 Dh10/free; 🕑 9am-5pm Wed-Mon)

**Sleeping** Palais Didi ( ☎ 035 558590; www.palaisdidi.com; 7 Dar Lakbira, Ville Ancienne; r/ste €120/150); Ryad Bahia ( ☎ 035 554541; www.ryad-bahia.com; Derb Tiberbarine, Ville Ancienne; r €50-60, ste €80-90)

**Eating** Collier de la Colombe ( ☎ 035 555041; 67 Rue Driba, Ville Ancienne; meals from Dh151-300); Le Dauphin ( ☎ 035 523423; 5 Ave Mohammed V, Ville Nouvelle; meals from Dh151-300)

# VOLUBILIS & MOULAY IDRISS

This trip encompasses both the pagan and the pious. Volubilis was one of the most remote outposts of the Roman Empire, and today is the best-preserved archaeological site in Morocco. The town of Moulay Idriss was named for the country's most revered saint, who was a descendant of the Prophet and the founder of the country's first imperial dynasty. Together, these destinations make an easy and extremely enjoyable day trip from Fez.

A Unesco World Heritage site (one of only eight in Morocco), Volubilis was settled by Carthaginian traders in the 3rd century BC. Annexed by the Romans around AD 40, it was home to nearly 20,000 people in its heyday and was famed for being one of the empire's most important breadbaskets. Abandoned by the Romans around AD 280, it was inhabited until the 18th century, when its marble was plundered for Moulay Ismail's palace in Meknès.

The ruins are spectacularly sited in the middle of a huge plain. The **capitol**, **basilica**, **forum** and **triumphal arch** are prominently located, but the site's excellent mosaics can be more difficult to find. Make sure you seek out the **Labours of Hercules** and **Nymphs Bathing** mosaics near the House of the Knight, and don't miss the erotic **Abduction of Hylas by the Nymphs** and **Diana Bathing** mosaics in the House of Venus.

## INFORMATION
**Location** 67km northwest of Fez.
**Getting there** Most of the hotels in Fez will be able to organise a car and driver to take you to Volubilis and Moulay Idriss for the day. You can even stop in Meknès for a couple of hours on the same trip. This should cost approximately Dh800 for the day, regardless of how many people are in the car.
**Volubilis** (admission Dh10, guide per hr Dh 120; ☼ 8am-6pm) Parking charge negotiated with attendant.
**Moulay Idriss** Guide approximately Dh40.
**Essentials** A hat, water and sunscreen.
**Eating** There is a raft of cheap eateries on Moulay Idriss' main street where you can score a tasty meal for less than Dh50.

Approximately 4.5km from Volubilis, the whitewashed town of Moulay Idriss is one of Morocco's most revered pilgrimage sites (see p24). Its mosques and shrines are off-limits to non-Muslim visitors, but if you wander around a local guide is almost certain to offer to lead you through the winding and steep streets and up to one of the town's panoramic vantage points.

A walk back in time at the ancient Roman city of Volubilis

# >SNAPSHOTS

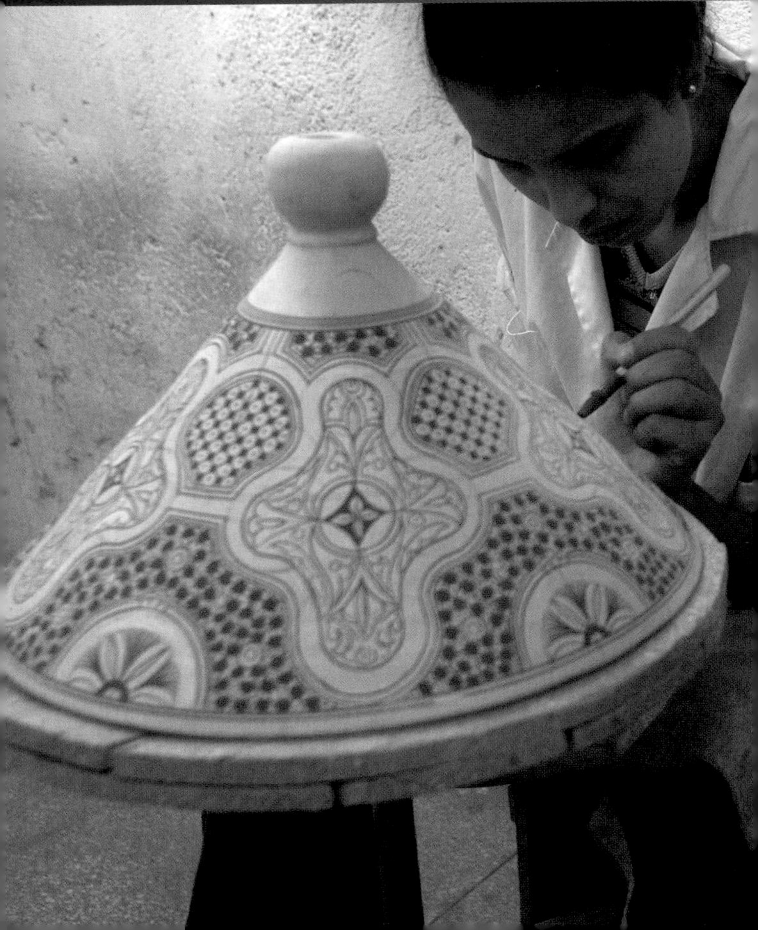

Fez is a city that enraptures both the soul and the senses. Its architectural riches are on a par with its vibrant music scene and fascinating Sufi heritage, and its artisans and cooks have honed their considerable and sometimes arcane skills over lifetimes. All of this makes a visit here supremely satisfying.

No ordinary brush-off – an artisan at work in a ceramics factory (p106)

# ACCOMMODATION

Fez certainly punches above its weight when it comes to sleeping options. Despite being a relatively small city, it offers an ever-growing and extraordinarily impressive range of *maisons d'hôtes* (small hotels), most of which are housed in charming riads (traditional houses built around gardens with trees) and *dars* (traditional houses with internal courtyards) in the medina. Both these types are generically referred to as 'riads'. There aren't many slick five-star choices in Fez, and if you're the type of traveller who craves swimming pools, breakfast buffets and a choice of cocktail bars, your only options are the overpriced and underwhelming **Sofitel Palais Jamais** (www.sofitel.com) and **Les Merinides** (www .lesmerinides.com) in the medina, and the **Crown Palace** (www.crownpalace.ma) in the Ville Nouvelle.

If you want a clean and comfortable three-star option that offers excellent value for money, **Hotel Batha** ( ☎ 035 6348240) in the medina or **Hotel Menzeh Zalagh** (www.menzeh-zalagh.ma) in the Ville Nouvelle both fit the bill. However, the rooms in these places are devoid of any character and have certainly seen better days.

Though there are a number of accommodation options in the Ville Nouvelle, we can't in good faith suggest staying there. There are simply no hotels impressive enough to lure you away from where all of the major sights of the city are – namely, the medina. Even more compelling is the fact that the riads in the medina encapsulate what Fez is all about – great architecture, stylish surrounds, warm welcomes and wonderful food.

Most of the riads are small, and offer 10 rooms or fewer. Some have their own hammams and/or spas, for example Riad Maison Bleue, Riad ibn Battouta, Riad Les Oudayas, Riad Fes); and others are known for their excellent cuisine, including Dar Anebar, Dar Roumana, Riad Lune et Soleil, Riad Les Oudayas, Riad Maison Bleue, Riad Fes, Riad Souafine and Riad Mabrouka.

Many of the riads also have comfortable terraces where you can relax while looking over the medina – listening to the sunset call to prayer from one of these will be a highlight of your stay. The best terraces are at Riad Fes, Riad Charqi, Dar Cordoba, Ryad Mabrouka, Dar Seffarine, Dar Roumana and Riad Souafine.

In terms of value for money, Dar Seffarine, Lune et Soleil, Riad Charqi, Dar el-Hana and Dar Iman are the standout choices.

If you're travelling as a family or group, you may want to stay in an apartment rather than a hotel. Fortunately there are plenty of beautifully restored riads available for rent; three of the best are **Pasha Baghdadi Massriya** (www.fesmedina.com), **Dar Aqiba** (www.discoverfez.com) and **Dar Bennis** (www.houseinfez.com).

A word of warning if you're planning to be in Fez during winter: riads can be very cold and they rarely have central heating installed. All have some type of heating, but if you feel the cold you may need to consider a five-star or Ville Nouvelle alternative.

It's possible to book all of the places we have listed direct, or you can rely on the highly regarded booking service offered by **Fez Riads** (www.fez-riads .com). This is run by Helen Ranger, the coauthor of this book, who donates a percentage of all booking costs to finance and manage much-needed public restoration projects in the medina. Helen has not been involved in the research and writing of this accommodation section to ensure there was no conflict of interest between her business and Lonely Planet's coverage.

Also check http://lonelyplanet.com/hotels (choose Africa as your destination, click on Morocco, then Fez).

## BEST HOSPITALITY
> Dar Anebar (www.daranebar.com)
> Dar Roumana (www.darroumana.com)
> Riad Lune et Soleil (www.luneetsoleil .com)
> Riad ibn Battouta (www.riadibn battouta.com)

## BEST STYLISH SURROUNDS
> Dar Seffarine (www.darseffarine.com)
> Riad Laaroussa (www.fez-riads.com /riad__laaroussa.htm)
> Riad Les Oudayas (www.lesoudayas .com in French)
> Riad Norma (www.riadnorma.com)

## BEST LUXE RETREATS
> Riad Fes (www.riadfes.com)
> Riad Maison Bleue (www.maison bleue.com)

## BEST SERVICE
> Dar Cordoba (www.darcordoba.com)
> Riad al-Bartal (www.riadalbartal.com)
> Ryad Mabrouka (www.ryadmabrouka .com)
> Riad Souafine (www.riadsouafine.com)

## BEST CHEAP-ISH SLEEPS
> Riad Charqi (www.riadcharqi.com)
> Dar Iman (http://fes-hostel.com)
> Dar el-Hana (www.darelhana.com)

# ARTISANS

The growth of craftsmanship and artistry is tied to the history of Fez. As the city grew outwards from the Kairaouine Mosque, each craft found its own area, and this is still seen today: on Talaa Kebira, carpenters still work at Nejjarine and metal workers can be found in the Seffarine district.

Tanners are organised in guilds and their work has hardly changed over hundreds of years – they still stand knee-deep in pits of cow urine, pigeon poo and other chemicals to clean the hides, cure and dye them (look for the hides drying in the cemetery above Bab Guissa). The hides supply the large market of leather goods: belts, jackets, bags, pouffes, drums, lanterns.

Slipper-makers are concentrated around the tanneries and make millions of pairs a year – yellow or white leather for men; every other colour under the sun for women, velvet or leather, embroidered or plain, with heels or without – that are mostly sold in the *kissariat* (covered markets) on Talaa Kebira. Dyed skins are also stretched over wrought-iron frames and decorated with henna to make lamps and hand-drums. There's a large industry for leather clothing and most outlets will make to order.

Decorated brassware and silver-plated metalware is very popular for teapots and trays, and the traditional area for this work is Seffarine. Copper-workers also operate here, tapping away at kettles, pots, basins and cauldrons. Lanterns made of pierced brass abound.

Passementerie – tassels, braiding and trimmings – has always been important: spinning thread of every hue for embroidered slippers, wedding belts, caftans and the tiny buttons that adorn jellabas.

To this day women embroider household linen by hand, using embroidery hoops. In antique shops, you'll see examples of old embroidery so fine that you fear for the craftswomen's eyesight. Look carefully into the tiny workshops on Talaa Kebira and you will spot basket weavers, hammam bucket-makers (see p53), sieve makers (to sieve sand for the sand and lime traditionally used in house construction), carpenters and wood turners making *mashrabiya* (intricate carved wood) screens, boxes, window frames and doors, and blacksmiths hammering curly wrought-iron window screens. There is just one man left making straw mats for the mosques (see p60) – his sons have set their sights on other careers.

The potteries – with their plumes of black smoke from the olive pits burned in the kilns – have been moved from the central to the outer medina at Ain Nokbi, but they still produce the traditional blue-glazed ceramics of Fez, from huge urns to bowls, plates and tajines, as well as multicoloured tiles cut by hand by *zellij maâlems* (mosaic-tilework masters) to cover walls and floors, fountains and table-tops.

One look inside a traditional building will get you wondering how many craftsmen produced the exquisite decorations. *Maâlems* were employed to create myriad patterns in tiny mosaics, others to carve plaster and *mashrabiya* screens, yet others to carve and paint cedarwood, and to apply plaster and *medluk* (fine sand-and-lime coating), the traditional finish of such grand buildings as the Kairaouine. Even the massive nails that stud doors are handcrafted. Craftsmen, in great demand for restoration projects, are a dwindling resource. Attempts are being made to keep the trades alive by such centres as the Institute of Traditional Building Crafts at Riyad Mokri (see p49). Fez remains a craft centre, and the Fassis know it's important now to retain this knowledge. Initiatives such as the proposed refurbishing of *funduqs* (caravanseries) to house craftsmen, with funding from the Millenium Challenge Corporation, will go a long way towards supporting these ancient arts; see p119 for more information.

### BEST CRAFT VIEWING

> Chouwara Tanneries (p42)
> Seffarine Sq for metalwork (p50)
> *Zellij* (mosaic tilework) at Art Naji (p87)
> Bucket-making (p53)
> Woodworking (p64)
> Straw mat–making (p60)

### BEST CRAFT SHOPPING

> Embroidery at Neq Broderie (p60)
> Bags galore at the Cooperative Artisanale/Leatherworker's Cooperative (p56)
> *Babouches* (slippers) at the *kissariat* (covered markets) (p58)
> Ceramics at Maison Bleue (p59)
> No-nonsense terracotta tajines at Chez Boutbi Nadia (p55)

### BEST BUILDING CRAFTS

> Nejjarine Museum for woodwork (p48)
> *Mashrabiya* (intricate carved wood) panels at Sagha Funduq (p49)
> Carved plaster at the Bou Inania Medersa (p41)
> The *zellij* at the Attarine Medersa (p38) and Bou Inania Medersa (p41)
> Nejjarine Fountain (p48)
> The painted wood at Moulay Idriss Zawiya (p48)

### BEST RESTORED BUILDINGS

> Dar Seffarine (p104)
> The *funduq* (caravanserai) housing the Nejjarine Wood Museum (p48)
> Dar Adiyel (p42)
> Kairaouine Mosque (p47)

# EATING & DRINKING

Words can't do justice to the experience of cutting into a pigeon b'stilla (savoury-sweet pie made with fine pastry) and having its heady aromas of cinnamon, allspice and ginger engulf the table. This famous dish, known for its unexpected melding of sweet and salty flavours and its perfectly balanced smooth and crisp textures, is an example of everything that is most wonderful about Moroccan cuisine – meltingly tender meat, aromatic and flavourful ingredients, and presentation that is both theatrical and drop-dead gorgeous. Like many Fassi dishes, b'stilla has its roots in Andalusia – it was from that part of Spain that ingredients such as olives, nuts, almonds, oranges and plums came and where the savoury-sweet technique was forged. These ingredients and many others have been absorbed into the national cuisine, enriching favourites such as couscous (fluffy semolina served with slow-simmered beef, chicken or vegetables; traditionally served on Fridays), m'choui (spiced roast lamb), harira (a thick, often lamb-based, pulse soup flavoured with tomato, onion, parsley and coriander and finished with a squeeze of lemon), tajines (slow-cooked, highly flavoured stews of meats, veg and/or fruit cooked in conical earthenware pots over coals) and kefta (spiced minced lamb served as kebabs or in tajines). Vegetarian versions of these dishes are not uncommon; the traditional first course of a huge array of cooked salads is almost always vegetarian.

You'll be able to sample all of these dishes and many others while in Fez, and should aim to do so in at least one of the restaurants we've mentioned (see opposite). Make sure you sample some of the street food, too – snail soup, brochettes (kebabs) and kefta sandwiches are delicious and dangerous in equal parts (consider yourself warned), but roasted corn and freshly baked doughnuts, Moroccan pancakes and pastries stuffed with khlia (strips of mutton preserved in fat) are safe and oh-so-tasty. Also fabulous are b'sara (broad-bean purée with cumin, olive oil and a sprinkle of paprika) slathered on freshly baked *khoobz* (flat bread), and the delicate *cornes de gazelle* (horn-shaped pastry filled with almond paste, dipped in orange water and dusted with sugar).

To accompany your meals, there are plenty of tipples on offer. Freshly squeezed *aseer limoon* (orange juice) is available everywhere, as is sweet and scented *thé b'na na* (mint tea) and *qahwa* (coffee). Moroccan coffee is strong, short and served with spices; it can be ordered with sugar *(wa sukkar)*, or without *(bla sukkar)*; if you want a French-style cup, ask for *café noir* (black) or *café au lait* (with milk).

Though Morocco is a Muslim country, there is an excellent range of local wine to choose from. A legacy of the French Mandate, the country's vineyards (60% of which are located around Meknès and Fez) produce extremely quaffable vintages from 14 Appellations d'Origine Garantie (AOG) and one Appellation d'Origine Contrôlée (AC). Stand-out products include Médaillon Sauvignon Blanc and Cabernet Sauvignon; Les Coteaux de L'Atlas 1er Cru Rouge and Blanc; S de Siroua Cabernet Sauvignon, rosé and Syrah; and Le Val d'Argan's El-Mogador red and white. Note that poor transport and cellaring of wine here can mean that the spoil rate is relatively high – if you encounter a spoiled bottle don't be afraid to send it back. The local lager is Flag Special, and you can also sometimes also order Casablanca.

If you're a fanatical foodie you might like to do a cookery course while you're in town. The affable **Lahcen Beqqi** (www.fescooking.com) runs half-day classes from the kitchen of Riad Tafilalet in the medina – he'll take you shopping in the Ville Nouvelle's Central Market (p90) first and then cook a delicious lunch for you while you watch and (very occasionally) assist. The excellent chefs at **Riad Souafine** (www.riadsouafine.com) and **Dar Roumana** (www.darroumana.com) both run classes that are more hands-on.

| BEST MOROCCAN FOOD | BEST CAFÉS |
|---|---|
| > Dar Anebar (p65) | > Assouan (p93) |
| > Dar el-Ghalia (p65) | > Café Kortoba (p69) |
| > La Maison Bleue (p65) | > Café de Tabarakallah (p69) |
| > Riad Fes (p67) | > Cremerie la Place (p69) |
| > Restaurant Zagora (p92) | |

**Top left** Nougat nuggets (p61)

# SUFISM

There's a strong tradition of Sufism in Morocco. As the country's spiritual capital, Fez is where the visitor is most likely to come across Sufi brotherhoods in procession through the streets on the Prophet's birthday or in musical ceremonies.

Described by 15th-century Sufi master and writer Sheikh Ahmad Zarruq as 'a science whose objective is the reparation of the heart and turning it away from all else but God', Sufism is the mystic tradition of Islam and a pathway to enlightenment.

The *tariqas* (brotherhoods) are led by sheikhs, revered figures giving guidance to followers who can number in the millions. The Tariqa Tijaniya, whose founder Sidi Ahmed Tijani lies buried in the medina (see p50), is probably the most important brotherhood in Fez.

At events such as the Fes Festival of Sufi Culture (p22) and the Fes Festival of World Sacred Music (p12), brotherhoods perform *dhikr* (awareness of God through the repetition of divine names) and *samaa* (worship with music and dance). As the intensity of the music increases, the group (and often the audience) start to sway in time to the prayers. The ceremony can lead to *hadhra* (feeling the presence of God), causing the participants to fall into a trance. The Hamadcha Brotherhood's website has interesting video footage: www.hamadcha-fez.com.

Some brotherhoods perform at weddings and parties, but they don't necessarily need a particular reason. 'Our faith is a gift of God,' says Sheikh Mouad al-Qadir Boudchiche of the Tariqa Qadiriya Boudchichiya. 'But singing is not the object – the aim is to meet the face of God.'

Meeting the face of God: a Sufi *tariqa* (brotherhood) aims for the divine

# MUSIC

Get into the music and discover the heart of Fez. The streets reverberate with music, whether it's boys drumming plastic bottles, professional musicians performing at a wedding or the muezzin's call to prayer five times per day.

The classical forms of Andalus and Malhoun are both found in Fez. Andalus was brought from Spain with the Moors, but has its origins in Iraq. Singers perform religious or secular poetry and the orchestra plays the *rbab* (fiddle), *oud* (lute), *kamenjah* (violin played vertically), *qanun* (zither), *darbuka* (goblet drum) and *taarija* (tambourine).

If Andalus is slightly stiff, Malhoun is livelier and much more a music of ordinary people. The orchestra plays the same instruments, with the addition of *swisen* (a small lute), *hadjouj* (bass lute) and *handqa* (small brass cymbals). Women have now started to sing Malhoun too.

Sufi brotherhoods use music to get closer to God (see opposite). They play and chant the names of Allah, gradually working themselves into a trance, and can be found at healing ceremonies, house blessings, *moussems* (pilgrimages or festivals) and during Mouloud (the Prophet's birthday) celebrations.

Although from the south of the country, Gnaoua musicians can be seen in Fez, brightly dressed in satins with hats adorned with seashells and 'jewels', playing the *gimbri* (a type of lute) and *garagab* (metal castanets).

Mix these classical forms with Berber music and add elements of anything from Western pop, flamenco, reggae, hip-hop or house, and fusion is born, taking Moroccan music into the future.

Check out what's happening at www.riadzany.blogspot.com.

## BEST MUSIC FESTIVALS
> Fes Festival of World Sacred Music (p12)
> Fes Festival of Sufi Culture (p22)
> National Festival of Andalus Music in Fes (p22)
> Festival of Malhoun Music (p23)

## BEST LIVE MUSIC
> Sufi Nights at the Fes Festival of World Sacred Music (p12)
> Moussem of Moulay Idriss (p24)
> La Maison Bleue (p65)
> Fusion music at concerts sponsored by the American Language Center (☎ 035 624850) or the French Institute (☎ 035 623921)

# HERITAGE FEZ

The medina of Fez was the first site in Morocco to be added to the World Heritage List. That was back in 1981, and since that time **ADER** (Agency for the Dedensification & Rehabilitation of the Fez Medina; www.aderfes.ma), has been the major player in the push to implement a programme of safeguarding and rehabilitating this living and breathing time capsule. ADER has sponsored major projects such as the restoration of the medina's historic ramparts (currently underway), as well as embarking upon targeted projects such as distributing Dh20 million in assistance grants towards private restoration of architecturally important but structurally unsound buildings.

ADER's working brief is wide ranging – for instance, it also works on projects to improve working conditions for artisans in the medina – and one of its greatest challenges is raising sufficient funds to deliver its many programmes. With Unesco's help, director-general Fouad Serrhini spends a lot of his time fundraising with private corporations and foreign governments. Major successes in this area have included the Arab Fund for Economic & Social Development's Dh50 million funding of the restoration of fountains, sewers and watercourses throughout the medina, the restoration of Bab Makina, and the painstaking restoration of the Attarine Medersa.

One of ADER's most important and resource-consuming tasks is its GIS mapping and documentation of the medina; 30 ADER technicians currently pound the pavement every day identifying and prioritising restoration projects. To date they have identified 14,000 buildings in need of attention, 9000 of which are houses and 1200 of which are currently scaffolded for safety reasons.

Sieve maker (p106) working in his shop

Decorative door to the Kairaouine Mosque (p47)

# BACKGROUND

## HISTORY

On first entering the medina of Fez you will be forgiven if you think that you've stepped back in time. This ochre city, lying in a bowl of mountains at the foot of the Middle Atlas, looks and feels as it has for centuries. There might be satellite dishes and cybercafés, but they make no impact on the all-encompassing feeling of being inside a medieval time-capsule.

Fez has a history peppered with political intrigue and upheaval, public resistance and pervasive individuality. The settlement has always been strategically and economically important, for it lies in fertile countryside along the caravan routes from the Sahara to the coast.

After the death of the Prophet in AD 632, the Arabs set out to take Islam into Africa and beyond. Moulay Idriss I, descendant of the Prophet Mohammed, came to this part of North Africa and settled in the former Roman city of Volubilis in the late 700s. He was accepted by the local Berber tribes as imam (religious leader), and therefore ruler (still a requirement of present-day monarchs). He soon found Volubilis too small and wanted to develop nearby Fez, but was assassinated before he could achieve this. It was left to his son Moulay Idriss II to fulfil his father's dream of a new capital, and he established the city in AD 809. Not one to endure living on a building site, he stayed in nearby Sefrou for the duration. His tomb, the Moulay Idriss *zawiya* (shrine), lies at the heart of Fez near the Kairaouine Mosque and is the most revered place of pilgrimage in all Morocco.

The city grew with the arrival in AD 818 of Muslim refugees from Al-Andalus in Spain who settled on the east bank of the Oued Fès (Fez River), and others a few years later from Kairouan in present-day Tunisia who set up home on the west bank of the river. The Kairaouine Mosque & University were established in AD 859 by Fatima and Meryem al Fihria, daughters of refugees, and Fez became a seat of great learning as well as a politically and commercially important city. Fassis are rightly proud of their heritage and there were a number of important thinkers who studied or lived in the city, such as the great Jewish philosopher Maïmonides who taught at the Kairaouine University; the Sufi philosopher from Andalucia Ibn al-Arabi; lawyer, philosopher and historian Ibn Khaldun; and Sylvestre II, pope from 999 to 1003, who later introduced Arabic numerals to Europe.

The Idrissids, the first of the Arab dynasties, was followed by two Berber ones: in 1069 the Almoravid sultan Youssef ben Tachfin was credited with joining the two separate parts of the city by building one city wall. The city fell to the Almohads in 1147. By the turn of the century, Fez had 120,000 residents, boosted by Muslim and Jewish refugees from Spain. Known for its silk, leather and metalwork, the city expanded and enjoyed an economic boom.

The Merinids ruled from 1248–1554, and made Fez their capital. Today their tombs, high on the hill to the north of the medina, look out over their achievements. This was greatest period of development: Fes el-Jdid (New Fez) was built, housing the palace, court and administrative buildings, and the Jews were moved here around this time. The Merinids refurbished the Moulay Idriss *zawiya* in 1437. The glorious *medersas* (theological colleges) such as Attarine, Sahrij, Bou Inania and Seffarine date from this dynasty. Craftsmen and their guilds abounded. The Merinids supported learning and culture, and were patrons to historians Ibn Khaldun and Leo Africanus, and the great traveller Ibn Battuta.

Into this cultural and religious mecca came exotic goods from the Arab world and sub-Saharan Africa, such as gold, silk, frankincense and spices. Fez saw many caravans passing through. They would put up at the *funduqs* (caravanseries), many of which were built in the Merinid period. Camels and horses would be stabled nearby, merchants would sleep in the rooms around the 1st-floor balcony, and goods would be traded in the courtyard on the ground floor. These *funduqs*, with their sometimes beautiful decoration, are still to be found in the medina.

But all this culture and commerce and having it so good couldn't last for ever. In 1549 the Saadians came thundering out of the Drâa Valley in the south to protect their desert trade routes against the Portuguese marauding the coast. This new dynasty didn't care much for Fez and its troublous population, and made Marrakesh its capital, but it did build fortifications around Fez, such as the Borj Nord and Borj Sud. The Saadians had a hard time controlling the north of the country. Fez fell into a period of unrest and poverty until Moulay Ismail, the second ruler of the Alawite dynasty, took control in 1672 and reigned for 55 years, making Meknès his capital. He was successful in uniting the country, although he was a bloodthirsty, extravagant tyrant.

The Alawites (who still reign today) embarked on a programme of building more *medersas* and mosques and restoring other buildings, but the coastal towns became more important economically.

Enter the French. In 1912 Sultan Moulay Hafid signed the Treaty of Fès which gave the French the right to defend Morocco. Subduing the city took a while, and they soon realised that Rabat would make a more convenient capital. The French built the Fez Ville Nouvelle in the 1920s and left the medina to itself, a policy that thankfully was followed throughout the country.

While France built towns, roads, dams and railways, and 'pacified' much of the country, they also educated the natives, hoping for allies in the Moroccan middle-class. Fez, however, became a hotbed of nationalism pressing for independence, and it was here that the Istiqlal (Independence) Party was formed in 1943. Within eight years the party had 100,000 members and was strongly supported by Sultan Mohammed V. Riots broke out and forced the French to act, and the sultan was exiled to Madagascar in 1953. More violence erupted and French settlers were at risk; eventually the French had no option but to grant independence to Morocco in 1956 and allow the exiled ruler, now King Mohammed V, to return.

At independence, French settlers returned to France, leaving their large airy villas in the Ville Nouvelle. The Jewish population also left in large numbers; many to Israel, some to France and others just as far as Casablanca. This gave many of the Moroccan elite and middle classes the opportunity to move from the medina and embrace a more modern way of life. Replacing them, rural people came seeking jobs in the city and set up home in the houses of the medina, sometimes several families living in one house.

King Mohammed VI succeeded to the throne on his father's death in 1999. The young king married a Fassi, Princess Lalla Salma, and they now have two children, Crown Prince Hassan and Princess Lalla Khadija.

## LONG LIVE THE KING

King Mohammed VI, a sherif (descendant of the Prophet), is an 'executive monarch' looking to reform his country and provide a link between the Arab world, Africa and Europe. The penal code, press code and labour laws have been reformed under his rule, but his most sweeping action was the introduction of the Mudawanna (new family code) in 2004. This promotes gender equality through the law and family courts have been established to deal with matters previously dealt with by religious clerics.

Elections in September 2007 were deemed fair but only attracted a 37% turnout due to general disillusionment. The moderate Islamist Justice & Development Party didn't do as well as expected. Thirty-three parties competed, with the Istiqlal Party coming out on top – but all power remains with the royal palace.

# LIFE AS A FEZ RESIDENT

The Fez medina might look medieval, but it's no theme park. It's the largest traffic-free conurbation in the world and was chosen as the Islamic World's City of Culture in 2007. Each community has at least one mosque with an accompanying fountain, as well as a *medersa*, a hammam and a communal bakery. Unemployment is high (officially 20%), which is why you see so many men hanging around in cafés making a glass of coffee last hours. If they do have work in the medina, it will probably be in one of the crafts or shops. If they work in the Ville Nouvelle, they'll have to walk to a bus stop to get into town.

Women rarely work outside the house, but housework is real drudgery. While virtually all houses in the medina have cheap running water these days, some families would still rather draw free water from the public fountains; that means a trip down the street with buckets. They might have a fridge, but they won't have a washing machine. Meal preparation will entail squatting on the floor to chop and cooking on a brazier or gas burner with a tajine on top. Houses rarely have bathrooms; there'll be a squat toilet next to the kitchen and a weekly trip to the hammam on Thursday or Friday. As the main meal of the day is lunch, the women start preparing early in the day. First there's a trip to the market and then it's time to make bread. Once the dough is ready, they'll send their menfolk or children off to the *farranes* (communal ovens) with a tray of flat round loaves. After lunch there's a bit of a siesta, then the men return to work (or the café) and the children to school, which leaves plenty of time for Egyptian soaps on TV, among the other chores. Once the family's home again, there's a promenade on the streets around 6.30pm, a chance to meet friends and gossip and let the children play outside. Then it's back for dinner.

Along with religion, family is the most important tenet of Moroccan life. Fez being pretty conservative, children usually stay at home until they marry – early twenties for women, early thirties for men. Even then they might live at home if they're not earning enough to move out. Social interaction is often family-based and holidays, both religious and summer, are spent *en famille*.

Teenagers in the Ville Nouvelle are freer than those in the medina. Even so, Fez offers them little in comparison with other Moroccan cities. They can play sports at clubs, go to an internet café to chat online, attend activities at the various cultural centres, or go to a café with friends

(McDonald's is a favourite hang-out), but they must be home for dinner around 9pm. Once a little older, and if still unmarried, they might go to a café or a restaurant and stay out a bit later. By comparison, there are simply no facilities in the medina for teenagers. Any self-respecting girl would never be seen unaccompanied on the street after sundown, though the boys play football in the streets, or pool in the tiny shops that serve as pool halls.

Life in the Ville Nouvelle of Fez is completely different and more closely resembles life in any other medium-sized city. There are supermarkets (but no shopping centres), restaurants, offices, schools and mosques. Around 700,000 of Fez's one million inhabitants live in the Ville Nouvelle. As people flock to the city from the countryside, there's a great deal of building going on, from high-rise apartment blocks to fancy villas on the outskirts of town. Middle-class and wealthy homes have all the trappings of Western materialism.

High on the hillsides overlooking the medina are poorer neighbourhoods where people live in concrete apartment blocks. Here the women still prepare food and cook squatting on the floor. All Moroccan homes have a *salon* where banquettes line the walls and the family eats at a low round table.

The long Ave Hassan II is the main street and has recently been revamped: it now sports palm trees and lawns, flowers and some remarkable fountains, and many Fassis spend their evenings enjoying the new landscaping and the sidewalk cafés.

## MEDINA ETIQUETTE
### Do
> take the opportunity to get to know Moroccans – they're friendly and warm and genuinely interested in you.
> bargain when you shop in the medina souks, but arguing over small amounts is going a bit far.
> tip people for good service: 10% is generous in a restaurant or café; a couple of dirhams for the little boy who shows you the way will be happily accepted.

### Don't
> eat, drink or smoke on the streets during Ramadan.
> wear skimpy clothes: baring lots of skin is out. There's no need to cover your head, but acknowledging the conservative culture of the medina will earn you respect.
> get amorous on the street: save kisses and hugs for when you're back in your guesthouse.

# RELIGION

Soaring minarets, shimmering mosaics, intricate calligraphy, the muez-zin's mesmerising call to prayer: much of what thrills visitors in Morocco today is inspired by the Moroccans' deep and abiding faith in Islam. One of the Abrahamic faiths and based on the teachings of the Old and New Testaments, Islam is built on the Five Pillars: *shahada,* the affirmation of faith in God and God's word entrusted to the Prophet Mohammed; *salat,* or prayer, ideally performed five times a day; *zakat* or charity, a moral obligation to give to those in need; *sawm,* the fasting practised during the month of Ramadan; and *haj,* the pilgrimage to Mecca that is the culmination of lifelong faith for Muslims.

Like many Muslim countries, Morocco is mostly Sunni. There are four main schools of thought among the Sunnis, emphasising different as-pects of doctrine. The one most commonly followed today in Morocco is the Maliki school. Historically this school has been less strict, with Maliki *qaids* (judges) applying the religious code according to local custom rather than the absolute letter of the law.

One local tradition is the custom of venerating *marabouts* (saints). *Ma-rabouts* are devout Muslims whose acts of devotion and professions of faith were so profound that their very presence is considered to confer *baraka* (grace), even after their death. Moroccans go out of their way to visit *ma-rabouts'* tombs and *zawiyas* (shrines) to seek solace for what ails them and to celebrate in regular *moussems* (pilgrimages or festivals). This practice has more to do with ancient Berber beliefs and Sufism than orthodox Islam.

Sufism, the mystical branch of Islam, is particularly important in Morocco (see p110). In Fez, the spiritual capital, there are several brotherhoods with large followings. The most important is the Tariqa Tijaniya with its base in the medina – the *zawiya* of Sidi Ahmed Tijani (p50), the founder of this brotherhood, is particularly beautiful – and devotees of this brotherhood are found all over central and north Africa and beyond. Music and trance play a large role in Sufism and brotherhoods are invited to play at wed-dings, house blessings, baby-naming ceremonies and circumcisions.

# MEDINA PRESERVATION

While there's a lot of building going on in the Ville Nouvelle, there's no room to build anything new inside the tangled maze of the medina. However, a lot of it's crumbling away and sometimes falls down. The Fez medina became a Unesco World Heritage site in 1981 and has since attracted some funding for its preservation from home and abroad. The Millenium Challenge Corporation (MCC) has recently awarded Morocco some US$687.5 million over five years to stimulate economic growth by increasing productivity and improving employment in high potential sectors such as tourism. Fez is to benefit from this grant to the tune of US$111.87 million for the Artisan & Fez Medina Project which seeks to enhance the links between the craft sector, tourism, and the city's rich cultural, historic and architectural assets. With access to modern production techniques, business management skills and microfunding, local craftsmen and women will be able to increase sales. A number of dilapidated *funduqs* have been earmarked for restoration for this project.

When it comes to historical monuments, some have already been restored, such as the Bou Inania Medersa (p41) and the Water Clock (p50) opposite. The Attarine Medersa (p38) and the Kairaouine Mosque (p47) are being restored too. Other grand buildings such as the Mokri Palace (p48)and Dar Ba Mohamed ben Chergui (p43) seem to have no hope of ever being saved and are sliding into gentle disrepair and decay as the sun blanches the paint from the doors and desiccates the wood, and weeds poke through the *zellij* (mosaic tilework). Perhaps the only hope of saving such grand houses is to allow them to be turned into luxury hotels.

There's a growing number of foreigners buying houses in the medina. This is a trend set to escalate (as are prices) as owners latch on to the fact that they can make some money out of the old family home and get themselves a shiny new apartment in the Ville Nouvelle. For the most part, the new Western owners are buying property inside the medina as holiday homes they can rent out or to turn into guesthouses. There are plans afoot too for large building projects (a 6.5-sq-mile site at Oued Fès),

## KNOCK KNOCK WHO'S THERE?

You won't see many windows on the outside of medina houses as it was the done thing to keep one's wealth (and women) out of sight. But on some houses you might spot a wooden half-barrel appendage about 3m or 4m up, with holes punched in it. If someone knocked at the door and the women of the house didn't know who it was, they could poke their head into the 'barrel', look through the holes, and drop a key down if they liked the look of their visitor. It's a sort of old-style door viewer, really, and saved them coming all the way downstairs.

a development near the golf course in the Ville Nouvelle, and two others on the hills around Fez, including holiday cottages with swimming pools, a conference centre, hotels, an artisan village and another golf course.

# ENVIRONMENT

The urban landscape of Fez, and indeed throughout Morocco, is not a pretty sight. Thin black plastic bags are ubiquitous with every small purchase and are strewn everywhere. Children and adults discard packaging without a thought and refuse clogs the rivers. Buses and taxis belch black exhaust fumes. Household rubbish is left on the streets to be collected and there is no recycling system. Donkeys and mules wear a kind of nappy, but there are still plenty of droppings to be avoided underfoot. However streets are swept and rubbish collected nightly, so the streets are remarkably clean every morning.

Several years ago the potteries for which the city is famous were moved outside the walls to Ain Nokbi, but Fez has grown to such an extent that they are now only just on the periphery. The kilns are fired with olive pits that produce a greasy black smoke on the horizon daily. Add to that the stench of the tanneries that are found throughout the medina, caused by the skins themselves and the use of pigeon droppings in the tanning process, and it can be seen that the city desperately needs to upgrade its environmental policies.

# ENERGY & WATER

People in the medina mostly cook on gas. It's a common sight to see donkeys or mules struggling their way through the tiny streets, laden with large numbers of gas tanks. Gas is reliable and cheap, and very often people use pressure cookers to save fuel. Electricity is expensive, so usually the only electrical appliances in the house will be a fridge and TV, and fluorescent lighting. These days many of the guesthouses are using solar-powered water heaters. The units don't make for a very pretty skyline, but it's a sensible way to go.

Less sensible is the misuse of water. Africa is drying up, and Morocco is no exception. Fez has historically been well-supplied with water and had an interesting hydraulic system feeding houses, hammams (which, incidentally, are an environmentally friendly way to keep clean) and public fountains throughout the medina. However, global warming and ecologically insensitive farming practices are putting a great strain on resources. An even greater strain is development investment-schemes with swimming pools and golf courses, which pander to tourists at the expense of the locals. While the authorities, aided by the Japanese government, are working hard to provide all rural people around Fez with potable water, the situation isn't helped by what might be deemed irresponsible developments around the city.

# FURTHER READING & RESOURCES
## BOOKS

**Dreams of Trespass: Tales of a Harem Girlhood** (Fatema Mernissi) Drawing on her own Fassi childhood memories and the dreams of the women surrounding her, Mernissi provides an imaginative story of a girl exploring the boundaries of time and place, gender and sex within the last 70 years.

**Fes Medina Tourist Circuits Guide** (ADER; Agency for the Dedensification & Rehabilitation of the Fez Medina; www.aderfes.ma) Colour-coded wall maps and explanations of various sites can be seen in the medina, and are accompanied by this book of self-guided walking tours of the medina.

**Fez, City of Islam** (Titus Burckhardt) Republished with the original 1930s black-and-white photographs as well as new ones, this masterpiece provides a profound understanding of Islamic history, culture and religion.

**Fez from Bab to Bab** (Hammad Berrada) Eleven different walks in the medina are described in this book, allowing the reader to discover unknown corners and courtyards in this labyrinth.

**House in Fez** (Suzanna Clarke) With feisty determination Clarke and her husband plunged into the process of restoring an old riad, an experience that veered between frustration, hilarity and moments of pure exhilaration. This book explores Moroccan culture, history and Islam, traditional Sufi rituals and the world of women.

**In Morocco** (Edith Wharton) In these memoirs of an American invited to tour Morocco in 1918 by the French resident-general Lyautey, Wharton's approach is somewhat patronising, but interesting for her impressions of markets, harems, palaces and mosques she visited.

**Leo the African** (Amin Maalouf) Maalouf spins a colourful tale based on the life of Hasan al-Wazzan who became known as Leo Africanus. Fleeing the Inquisition in Spain, this 16th-century traveller and writer spent his childhood and young adulthood in Fez, and the book paints a remarkable picture of life in the city at that time.

**Lords of the Atlas** (Gavin Maxwell) A riveting political intrigue centred on the Glaoui brothers from the south of Morocco, their ruthless rise to power and their subsequent sorry demise. Fez plays an important role as the city El-Glaoui could never quite conquer. (Note that Walter Harris's *Morocco That Was* is largely reproduced in the appendix of this book.)

**Morocco That Was** (Walter Harris) *The Times* correspondent in Morocco in the early part of the 20th century, Harris immersed himself in the local culture, befriending the royal family, as well as becoming involved in espionage for the British and French. He tells of his 35 years in Morocco with humour and perception.

**The Cobbler's Apprentice** (Sandy McCutcheon) With a theme of terrorism, counter-terrorism and bacteriological warfare, this thriller is partly set in the *babouche* (leather slipper) workshops and tiny alleyways of the Fez medina. A young Palestinian escapes from Guantanamo Bay and becomes an agent of mass destruction.

**The Spider's House** (Paul Bowles) Fez in the twilight of the French occupation is the arena for this political *tour de force* considered by many to be Bowles's finest. Daily Fez life, with its web-like complexities, provides a fascinating backdrop.

## INTERNET RESOURCES

**www.fesfestival.com** This is the official site of the Fes Festival of World Sacred Music, listing the programme and events.

**www.houseinfez.com** Has a mine of information on buying and restoring houses in the Fez medina.

**www.par-chemins.org** Check out this site for details of the Fes Festival of Sufi Culture, with its debates on Sufism in a world context and plenty of Sufi music.

**www.riadzany.blogspot.com** The View from Fez blog contains news, views and photographs of Fez, as well as details of upcoming events.

**www.visitfes.org** A good site, but unfortunately still only in French. It gives details of all cultural events happening in Fez.

# DIRECTORY
## TRANSPORT
### ARRIVAL & DEPARTURE
### AIR

At the time of research the only airlines flying into Fez were **British Airways** (www.britishairways.com) operated by GB Airways from London's Gatwick airport; **Ryanair** (www.ryanair.com) from London's Luton airport, Barcelona's Girona airport, Marseille airport and Frankfurt's Hahn airport; **jet4you** (www.jet4you.com) from Paris' Orly airport; **Atlas Blue** (www.atlas-blue.com) from Marseille airport; and **Royal Air Maroc** (www.royalairmaroc.com) from London's Heathrow airport, Paris' Charles de Gaulle airport and Casablanca's Mohammed V.

No airlines fly directly between Fez and Marrakesh.

### Arriving in Fez

**Fez airport** (Aeroport International Fès-Saïss; code FEZ; ☎ 035 524800; www.onda.org.ma in French) is in Saïss, 10km to the southwest of the city. A taxi to the medina from the airport costs from Dh120 to Dh150. Alternatively, you can catch an ONCA bus from the airport to the Ville Nouvelle (Dh3.60) and then a taxi from the Ville Nouvelle to the medina (Dh8).

### Arriving in Casablanca

If you are flying into **Casablanca airport** (L'Aéroport International Mohammed V; code CMN; www.onda.org.ma in French; ☎ 022 539040) you can organise

---

## CLIMATE CHANGE & TRAVELLING TO FEZ

Travel – especially air travel – is a significant contributor to global climate change. At Lonely Planet, we believe that all travellers have a responsibility to limit their personal impact. As a result, we have teamed with Rough Guides and other concerned industry partners to support Climate Care, which allows travellers to offset the greenhouse gases they are responsible for with contributions to energy-saving projects and other climate-friendly initiatives in the developing world. We also offset all of our staff and author travel.

Before you book an air ticket to Fez, look at the transport alternatives. If you are in Europe and you have enough time, you may like to investigate travelling here via train and ferry rather than by air. Thomas Cook publishes an Overseas Timetable (£12.50), or check the handy www.seat61.com website for train information. For ferry information, go to www.comarit.com in Spanish and French, www.comanav.ma in French, www.frs.ma, www.trasmediterranea.es and www.ferrimaroc.com.

For more information check out the responsible travel pages on www.lonelyplanet.com. For details on offsetting your carbon emissions and a carbon calculator, go to www.climatecare.org.

for your hotel in Fez to send a car to collect you. The trip between the airport and Fez usually takes 3½ hours. The cost of this service should be Dh1300, but some hotels charge a bit more.

The officially posted taxi fare from the airport to Fez is Dh1300 and taxis are almost always available to take passengers to Fez. Don't organise your taxi through one of the touts in the arrival hall, as this always costs more. Just make your own way to the rank outside the arrival hall.

Your other option is to go down the escalator from the arrival hall and catch the Aéroport Express shuttle train from the airport to Casablanca's Casa-Voyageurs train station (1st/2nd class Dh50/35, 36 minutes, 32 services per day from 6am to midnight) and then transfer to a Fez-bound service (1st/2nd class Dh155/103, four hours, 10 services per day from 6.15am to 10.15pm). You can buy a combined ticket for this from the ticket desk at the airport shuttle station. You'll then need to catch a taxi to the medina (Dh8) from the train station in Fez.

## TRAIN

A train line links Oujda in the east of the country with Fez, Meknès, Rabat, Casablanca and Marrakesh. See www.oncf.ma for schedule and price details.

The **train station** (Map p89, A1; ☎ 035 625001) is in the Ville Nouvelle.

## VISA

Most visitors to Morocco do not require visas and are allowed to stay in the country for 90 days on entry. Exceptions to this rule include nationals of Israel, South Africa and Zimbabwe. Check with the Moroccan embassy or consulate in your home country before travelling, as visa requirements can change.

Note that your passport must be valid for at least six months beyond your date of entry into Morocco.

## GETTING AROUND

The narrow, maze-like streets of the medina, Al-Andalous quarter and Fez el-Jdid dictate that the only practical way to get around is by foot. It's possible to catch a petit taxi (small red local taxi) from each gate along the ramparts and travel to another; many travellers end up walking from one point in the medina to another and then returning by petit taxi. The downhill walk from Bab Bou Jeloud, down Talaa Kebira, through Seffarine Sq and on to Bab R'cif is a perfect example of this.

To travel between the medina and the Ville Nouvelle, you can walk (about 40 minutes), catch a bus from Batha or R'cif, or catch a petit taxi.

## Transport Between Key Destinations

| Destination | Walk | Petit taxi | Bus |
|---|---|---|---|
| Medina (Batha)–Fez el-Jdid (Pl Alaouites) | 25min | 5min | |
| Medina (Batha)–Al-Andalous (Bab R'cif) | 25min | 8min | 10min |
| Medina (Batha)–Ville Nouvelle (Pl Yacoub Al Mansour) | 40min | 8min | 10min |
| Fez el-Jdid (Pl Alaouites)–Al-Andalous (Bab Fettouh) | | 10min | |
| Fez el-Jdid (Pl Alaouites)–Ville Nouvelle (Pl Yacoub Al Mansour) | 15min | 5min | 7min |
| Al-Andalous (Bab R'cif)–Ville Nouvelle (Pl Yacoub Al Mansour) | | 10min | 15min |

## PETIT TAXIS

The city is awash with petits taxis that will take you from one point to another quickly and cheaply. Fares are calculated by the meter (see table, right). There are loads of taxis in the Ville Nouvelle and you will almost always find taxis on the ranks at Batha, Ain Azleten and Bab R'cif in the medina; be warned though that at peak times (around 9am, at lunchtime and around 6pm) demand is high and snaffling an empty taxi from a rank or street can be a challenge of almost gladiatorial proportions. You'll need to pounce quickly, be assertive in staking your claim and wherever possible state your destination after getting into the cab rather than before (drivers can be loath to accept passengers wanting to take short trips).

Don't be surprised if on your journey the driver stops to take other passengers on board; this is accepted practice and both you and the extra passenger(s) will be expected to pay the full fare to your destination.

During Ramadan it's sensible to give up any ambition to catch

| Petit taxi route | Fare |
|---|---|
| Batha-Pl Alaouites | Dh6 |
| Batha-R'cif | Dh8-9 |
| Batha-Ville Nouvelle | Dh8-9 |
| R'cif-Ain Azleten | Dh12 |
| R'cif-Pl Alaouites | Dh9 |
| R'cif-Ville Nouvelle | Dh12 |
| R'cif-Ziat | Dh7 |

All fares are 50% higher after 8pm.

a taxi in the hour or so before or during *iftar* (the breaking of the day's fast at sunset).

## BUS

The local buses are dirty, uncomfortable and jam-packed. They also have a reputation for harbouring pickpockets. We suggest walking or catching a petit taxi as an alternative, particularly as the buses aren't all that much cheaper than a petit taxi (eg bus 8 between Batha and the Ville Nouvelle costs Dh3.50 whereas a petit taxi costs Dh8 to Dh9).

## DONKEY & MULE

Only joking.

# PRACTICALITIES

## BUSINESS HOURS

Business hours in the medina are different to those in the Ville Nouvelle. Shops, the medina souks and produce markets generally open from 9.30am to 12.30pm and 2.30pm to 8pm. Weekend opening hours are different depending on whether you're in the medina or the Ville Nouvelle. In the medina shops are often closed at prayer times and on Friday afternoon (sometimes all day Friday); in the Ville Nouvelle most shops and businesses stay open on Fridays but are closed on Saturday afternoons and Sunday.

Restaurants open from noon to 3pm and 7pm to 10pm daily. Café hours vary wildly, but they're generally open from 8am to 8pm Saturday to Thursday. Banks operate from 8.15am to 3.45pm Monday to Friday; post offices open from 8am to 4.30pm Monday to Friday and 9am to noon on Saturday.

During the holy month of Ramadan many cafés and restaurants close during the day, and opening hours generally can be hard to predict. In Fez non-Muslims are not allowed to enter mosques.

Daily opening hours are given unless stated otherwise. See also the inside front cover of this book.

## DANGERS & ANNOYANCES

It is not really safe for women to walk through the medina by themselves late at night. Hotels are usually happy to provide an escort if you request this.

Those travellers arriving by train from Casablanca should beware the hotel touts who work the train – don't automatically believe anyone who tells you that the hotel you have chosen is closed, dishonest, filthy or a brothel. Go and check for yourself. The same applies to visitors approaching the city by car; don't take any notice of the touts who will pull up beside you on a motorcycle and try to escort you to a hotel.

See also Guides (below).

## EMERGENCIES

For emergencies:

**All-night pharmacy** (Map p89, C1; Ave Moulay Youssef, Ville Nouvelle; ☎ 035 623380)
**Ambulance & Fire** ( ☎ 15)
**Hôpital el-Ghassani** (off Map p89; ☎ 035 622777/8/9; Dhar al-Mahrez)
**Police** ( ☎ 19)

## ELECTRICITY

Moroccan sockets accept the European round two-plug pin.

## GUIDES

Until recently, Fez was notorious for its *faux guides* (unofficial guides), who pounced upon tourists in the hope of picking up a few hours' guiding work. The authorities have recently cracked down on these guides, and are doing everything they can to ensure that official guides have a monopoly on this lucrative industry. There are two types of official guides: *guides nationaux* (guides accredited to work anywhere in Morocco) and *guides locaux* (guides accredited to work only in Fez). Their fees are set by the government: *guides nationaux* may charge Dh150 for a half day, Dh250 for a full day and Dh300 for a day trip outside town; *guides locaux* may charge Dh120 for a

half day, Dh150 for a full day and Dh200 for a day trip.

All official guides must carry an identification card specifying whether they are *nationaux* or *locaux*. Most will try and encourage you to shop – this is because they will be paid a commission on any purchases you make. If you're not interested in shopping, make this very clear to the guide at the start of the tour and agree to pay a higher fee to compensate (an extra Dh50 is fair).

All of the guides appreciate a tip at the end of the tour. This is totally at your discretion.

## HOLIDAYS

**New Years Day** 1 January
**Independence Manifesto** 11 January
**Labour Day** 1 May
**National Day (Amendment of the Constitution)** 23 May
**Throne Day** 30 July
**Oued Eddahab Allegiance Day** 14 August
**Revolution Day** 20 August
**King's Birthday** 21 August
**Commemoration of the Green March** 6 November
**Independence Day** 18 November

The following Islamic holidays are also celebrated (dates aren't confirmed until the new moon is sighted):
**Eid el-Adha** 10 December in 2008; 30 November in 2009
**Eid el-Mawlid** 20 March in 2008; 9 March in 2009

**Eid el-Fitr** 3 October in 2008; 20 September in 2009

The holy month of Ramadan will start around 2 September in 2008 and 22 August in 2009. During this month it's polite to avoid smoking, eating and drinking in the street.

## INTERNET

There are a reasonable number of internet cafés in the medina. Try **B@tha Net** (Map pp36-7, C5; per hr Dh10; 9am-10pm) in Derb Douh between Batha and Bab Bou Jeloud, or **Cyber Faiçal** (Map pp36-7, H6; per hr Dh5; 9am-10pm) opposite the Cinema Amal in R'cif.

There are more options in the Ville Nouvelle, one of the best being **CyberNet** (Map p89, C4; per hr Dh6; 9am-midnight) in Blvd Mohammed V.

Many of the hotels in the medina offer wi-fi.

For a list of useful websites see p123.

## LANGUAGE COURSES

**The Arabic Language Institute in Fez** (ALIF; Map p89, C2; ☎ 035 624850; www .alif fcs.com; 2 Rue Ahmed Hiba, Ville Nouvelle) is an affiliate of the well-regarded American Language Center. The language institute offers courses in Modern Standard Arabic or Colloquial Moroccan Arabic (six-/three-week courses Dh9400/5200). It can also organise private lessons.

## MONEY

There are plenty of ATMs in the Ville Nouvelle (especially on Ave Mohammed V), but not many in the medina and surrounding neighbourhoods. You'll find one machine in the Sociéte Générale Marocaine de Banques (SGMB) at Bab Bou Jeloud and another (Visa and MasterCard only) in the post office next to the Batha Museum; see Map pp36–7, C5. There are two ATMs near the Cinema Amal at Bab R'cif (Map pp36 7, G5) and one in the Banque Populaire just off Pl Alaouites in Fez el-Jdid.

There are currency exchange desks in the SGMB at Bab Bou Jeloud, the Banque Populaire (Map p75, C3) in Fez el-Jdid and in most of the banks on Blvd Mohammed V in the Ville Nouvelle.

Most shops and hotels will happily accept either euros or dirhams.

For exchange rates see the inside front cover.

## POST

If you're sending goods home, do so from the **central post office** (Map p89; cnr Ave Hassan II & Blvd Mohammed V, Ville Nouvelle) or use the reliable **Medina Express** ( ☎ 082 006060) service, which is offered by many reputable shops in the medina.

DIRECTORY

## TELEPHONE

Morocco has three GSM mobile (cell) phone networks: Méditel, Maroc Telecom and newcomer Wana. You can purchase a prepaid Moroccan mobile phone or SIM card at any *tabac* (tobacconist and newsstand) or *téléboutique* (private telephone office) – competition between the companies is fierce so special deals are frequently on offer. Méditel and Maroc Telecom also offer roaming agreements – you can check if your mobile phone company has an agreement with Méditel at the English page at www.meditel.ma /wm; Maroc Telecom doesn't list this information on its site – check the situation with your provider.

Moroccan mobile numbers start with the code ☎ 01, ☎ 06 or ☎ 07.

### COUNTRY & CITY CODES

**Fez** ( ☎ 035)
**Meknès** ( ☎ 035)
**Morocco** ( ☎ 212)

### USEFUL PHONE NUMBERS

**International direct dial code** ( ☎ 00)
**Local directory inquiries** ( ☎ 160)

## TIPPING

Tip waiters up to 10%; for taxis round up to the nearest dirham; and porters can be tipped Dh5 to Dh15 depending on how far they go.

## TOURIST INFORMATION

There's a **tourist information office** (Map p89, C4; ☎ 035 623460; fax 035 654370; Pl Mohammed V; ⏰ 8.30am-4.30pm Mon-Fri) in the Ville Nouvelle, but nothing in Fez el-Jdid, the medina and Al-Andalous.

The Conseil Régional du Tourisme de Fès (CRT) publishes the informative bimonthly *L'agenda Cultural de Fés et sa Région,* a free guide to all cultural events in the city and surrounding areas. It's distributed through most of the city's hotels; unfortunately it's in French only.

## TRAVELLERS WITH DISABILITIES

Fez is an extremely challenging destination for travellers with impaired movement or sight. Its streets are steep, winding and extremely narrow in parts, with uneven cobbles and lots of debris. None of the available public transport is accessible to people in wheelchairs, though we have known of disabled travellers who have hired donkeys to carry them around the medina. Discuss this with your hotel.

# >INDEX

*See also separate subindexes for See (p134), Shop (p135), Eat (p134), Drink (p134) and Play (p134).*

000 map pages

**000** map pages

### 🛒 SHOP

**000** map pages